REFLECTIONS ON THE GOSPELS

Reflections on the Gospels

Daily Devotions for Radical Christian Living

John Michael Talbot

SERVANT BOOKS
Ann Arbor, Michigan

Cover design: Michael Andaloro
Cover photograph: Edd Anthony, O.F.M.

Published by Servant Books
P.O. Box 8617
Ann Arbor, Michigan 48107

87 88 89 90 91   10 9 8 7 6 5 4 3

ISBN 0-89283-306-8
Printed in the United States of America

Note to the Reader

REFLECTIONS ON THE GOSPELS is designed to help the reader meditate on a gospel passage throughout the day. Some readers will be particularly interested to note that each reading corresponds to the daily gospel readings for the liturgical year. In fact, *Reflections on the Gospels* covers approximately one-third of the church year. It begins with the twenty-second week of Ordinary Time and continues through the Advent and Christmas seasons. For the Christmas feast itself, the reader is offered a rich fare of gospel readings from which to choose. Each reading is keyed to the liturgical year either by indicating the date or the particular week and day in Ordinary Time or Advent. For example, (22: Monday) at the head of the reading indicates that it is Monday, the twenty-second week in Ordinary Time. Whether or not you read *Reflections on the Gospels* in concert with the liturgical season, it is designed to bring you into contact every day with the living word of God.

Preface

I SHOULD WARN THE READER that this book is filled with gospel challenges and questions that are often directed at reputable Christian ministries, industries, and institutions. Please understand that I, myself, am involved in and with many of the entities that are challenged, so the questions are meant just as much for me as they are for anyone. As I read the words of Jesus every day, I am amazed at the fire that burns in them and am challenged and shaken to the core of my soul. I must admit that his words have burned away much of the mediocrity of my life which I propagated in his name.

Also, please understand that this book is not meant to be a calm and cool theological treatment of the topics mentioned. It is a devotional based on gospel texts. As such it often strongly emphasizes particular points to near overstatement in recognition that many other fine books already provide a balanced theological treatment of the same points. I do this prompted by the example of Jesus himself, who likewise evoked radical response in a religious environment by strongly emphasizing a particular truth. By doing this he cut through the rationalizations of the mind and pierced the human heart with the fire of the divine Spirit of God. I hope this devotional can do the same.

Just an Ordinary Man?
Luke 4:16-30 (22:Monday)

Jesus came to Nazareth where he had been reared, and entering the synagogue on the sabbath as he was in the habit of doing, he stood up to do the reading. (v. 16)

Jesus begins making the rounds through the synagogues to teach. He doesn't carry out his ministry in some big "show biz" fashion. He doesn't have books, doesn't make records or cassettes or tapes, hasn't any video cassette ministry. You don't see advertisements about him in the religious magazines or papers. He simply begins in the local church of his day, the synagogue.

However, this doesn't hinder him from proclaiming radical things. Even from the platform of ordinary religious ritual and conduct, Jesus proclaims a new spirituality that shakes the people of the synagogue to the core. Bring glad tidings to the poor. Set the captives free. Heal the sick and the blind. These are all radical challenges which shake our religion, moving it from mere externalism to a faith which heals the hurts of the world by the power of the Spirit within. Through Jesus, one of Nazareth's own local boys, the Spirit is being powerfully poured forth to announce a whole new year of favor, a whole new way of salvation.

Through all of this the ordinary is the vehicle for the extraordinary. Jesus was in a seemingly ordinary synagogue. Yet from this ordinary setting Jesus proclaims extraordinary things in the Spirit.

Jesus receives no better welcome here than he did later in Jerusalem. Here, as well as in Jerusalem, the crowd is at first curious, then confused, then so angry that they try to kill him. He proclaims great things, but is still unable to do many miracles because the people lack faith.

Are we able to both see and proclaim the extraordinary things of God in the midst of the ordinary things of this life? Do we limit our brother's and sister's potential to bring great healing into the world by our lack of faith? Do we pierce their hearts and crucify their enthusiasm through our own indifference? Or do we limit ourselves by thinking that the great things of God's Kingdom can only be accomplished through the "great things" of the world?

Let us begin to announce the salvation of Jesus within our own "synagogues": the local church, our own family, our friends and associates. These are the avenues for manifesting the greatness of Jesus' gospel to the poor. Let us do great things by simply loving the poor, the prisoner, and the afflicted of our imprisoned world. Then an outpouring of the Spirit will sweep across this country that will set it free from the shackles of materialism and greed.   □

Jesus Delivers Us
Luke 4:31-37 (22:Tuesday)

In the synagogue there was a man with an unclean spirit. (v. 33)

In many ways we respond to Jesus' words like the demons did: "Leave us alone! What do you want of us, Jesus of Nazareth? Have you come to destroy us? I know who you are: the Holy One of God."

Jesus speaks to us with authority, and we are spellbound by his teaching. Yet his words both attract and frighten us. They challenge us to the core of our being, and call us to reform and reshape our very soul according to his image.

We often resist this reformation of our life. We ask Jesus to just leave us alone. In near desperation we ask, "What do you want of us?" We know what he wants, and we know that once he takes control of our life we will never be the same. He will shake and uproot all the comfortable, cultural sins and habit patterns of darkness that we have embraced and nurtured since our youth. We want him to change the sins which bring us obvious despair, but we still hang on to many of our comfortable, "harmless" sins.

Jesus responds immediately to our whimpering: "Be quiet! Come out of him." He does not put up with the rationale of sin and darkness. He himself has battled the lies and deception of the devil's rationale during his own temptation in the wilderness (Lk 4:1-13), therefore, he speaks with the authority of personal experience. He does not even listen to the pathetic whimperings of our personal demons, nor should we. He acts quickly and decisively, commanding the demon to be quiet and to come out of our life. The demon obeys.

So Jesus speaks with authority and reshapes the image of our life to its very core and center. We often complain and question, but Jesus sees through our empty and superficial contentions. He silences our demons and casts them out. Our demons often "cast us to the ground," in a show of a temper and rage, but they finally "come out without doing us any harm." We find ourselves free of the little demons who have ensnared us for years. We find ourselves healed. Can we do anything but be "struck with astonishment" at the words of Jesus which reshape our whole life and cast out even our most "familiar spirits"?   □

Live Your Faith
Luke 4:38-44 (22: Wednesday)

All who had people sick with a variety of diseases took them to him, and he laid hands on each of them and cured them. Demons departed from many crying out as they did so. (v. 40-41)

The demons said, "You are the Son of God." All through Scripture it seems the demons are the first to recognize who Jesus really is. They call him "the Messiah, the Holy One of God," yet they remain demons.

So it is with us sometimes. We profess faith in Christ. We study theology, and attend seminars. We go to workshops and even participate in church programs. Yet our daily life remains unchanged.

As the Letter of James says, "Even the demons believe and shudder. Do you want proof, you ignoramus, that without works faith is idle?" It is not enough to just profess faith in Christ, we must live it!

Take as an example Peter's mother-in-law. As soon as she was touched by Jesus' healing, "she got up immediately and waited on them." Grace had an effect on her lifestyle as well as her words. She became a servant.

Jesus' touch must do the same for us. It is not enough to profess Christ with our lips without changing our life. It is not enough to receive the touch of Jesus' healing without becoming a servant of others.   ☐

Grace and Hard Work
Luke 5:1-11 (22:Thursday)

Master, we have been hard at it all night long and have caught nothing; but if you say so, I will lower the nets. (v. 5)

Often we work so hard and with seemingly few results; however, with the touch of grace, even a little effort becomes very fruitful. But it does take both effort and faith.

Peter was undoubtedly exhausted after working all through the night. And then Jesus came along and had the audacity to ask him to go back to work. Peter complains a little but in the end he lowers the nets and hauls in more fish than the nets can hold. Because of Peter's obedience, faith, and extra human effort, Jesus worked a miracle and proceeded to call Peter to become his disciple. It took human effort and faith for Peter to obey Jesus and lower the nets again, but it took the power of Jesus to work the miracle of filling Peter's net with fish.

Often, this is exactly the way Jesus works with us. He comes to us when we are tired and exhausted, when we have failed by relying on our own human effort. He asks us simply to trust him and try again according to his commands. If we trust and obey, we will see the kind of result that could easily be called a miracle.

We must never be possessive of the miraculous fruits of God's grace. Overwhelmed by the miracle, Peter humbly says to Jesus, "Leave me, Lord: I am a sinful man." In response Jesus instead calls Peter to leave everything, even the miraculous fish, and follow him to become a "fisher of men." With that Peter and his companion leave everything and become his followers.

When we witness the power of God and are called to such a faith commitment, we, like Peter, are often afraid. Jesus tells us, "Do not be afraid. From now on you will be catching men." □

Spirit-led Freedom
Luke 5:33-39 (22:Friday)

No one pours new wine into old wineskins. (v. 37)

What a contradiction this seems! These words defy, or burst, the wineskins of legalism or externalized religion. We can now "eat and drink freely" because Jesus is still with us through the Holy Spirit. Yet the groom has been removed from our midst and we "will surely fast in those days." We are free from the legalism of the law, yet we are called to fulfill and even surpass the precepts of the law in lived-out holiness.

This kind of Spirit-led freedom and radical holiness is difficult to contain within a legal religious system. The Spirit "blows where it will. You hear the sound it makes, but you do not know where it comes from or where it goes. So it is with everyone begotten of the Spirit." That is why Jesus says it will be difficult to pour the new wine of the covenant in his blood into the old wineskins of the law. It is so radical and so powerful in spirituality and holiness that it simply would burst the legal wineskins of the Old Testament law.

The new wineskin of the church will never burst, for it has been established to hold the wine of the Spirit and the blood of Jesus Christ. We are "built on the foundation of the apostles and the prophets with Christ Jesus as our cornerstone." The bishops and the pope are ordained successors. There is no new, New Testament church, for there is no new, New Testament. There is no new, New Testament because there is no new sacrifice of Jesus. There is no new sacrifice of Jesus because his blood has been shed on Calvary "once for all," and one Spirit has been given to all!

The moving of the Spirit still bursts many of our human structures within the church. They can, should, and do change. Today, the Spirit is raising up new communities and ministries that simply do not fit into the old structures. The communities and ministries are so radical and alive in the Spirit that they tend to burst the wineskins of the older, more established institutions within the church.

The zeal of the new is like a fire of the Spirit that burns up all that is not pure gold and silver within the old. The new communities often live the ideals of the old communities with new-found zeal in the Spirit, and challenge the old communities to return to their original ideals. Many of our old institutions must have their hay and stubble burned away with this new fire before their gold and silver will again be visible to the watching world. Jesus has come to "set a fire on the face of the earth." This fire is the daily working of the Holy Spirit.

As these new expressions are raised up by the Spirit in the church, most people still say: "I find the old wine better." The old communities and ministries have had hundreds of years to mature and mellow. Many times they not only mature and mellow, but they also cool off in zeal and become lukewarm in spirit. The new communities are zealous, but often inexperienced. We cannot deny that the authentic pouring out of the Spirit is likened not to the old, but to the new wine which needs the new wineskins of new structures to contain it. We have to be willing to become fools for Christ and children of the kingdom in order to be people of the Spirit. Given the years it needs to mature, this new wine will actually turn out just as good, if not better than the old.

What about our own life? Where are we unwilling to give up our old, comfortable ways in order to give place to the new working of the Spirit? Do we hang on to the security of old structures and lifestyles instead of stepping out in the faith which is willing to risk one's very life to be open to the work of the Spirit? We must continually die to the old if we are to be continually open to the new. This is an ongoing, daily process. We must continually question the old if we are to properly provide wineskins for the new wine. Otherwise, our comfortable security will burst, and we will be left with nothing. □

Jesus and the Law
Luke 6:1-5 (22:Saturday)

Why are you doing what is prohibited on the sabbath? (v. 2)

The saints of God are extraordinary people who are truly free. The Lord works through them to establish his laws on earth, then the people of the earth judge his chosen vessels when they don't conform to external legalisms of the law. But the heart of the law is spiritual, and the saints of God are people of the Spirit. As Paul says, "The spiritual man . . . can appraise everything, though he himself can be appraised by no one."

The law is given to serve God's people. God's people are not created to serve the law, but to love God. God's people are not for the law; the law is for God's people. Christian communities should exist only to bring people to God. The law is given to teach us basic truths which lead us to God. The law of God is misunderstood when it becomes the end or goal of our faith. Ironically, it becomes a false god. It ministers spiritual death rather than eternal life.

David broke a fine point of the law, but served God. Many people scrupulously observe all the fine points of the law, but are far from both God and their neighbors in their hearts. The more primary law of God is a love which feeds the hungry and poor in mercy. Jesus and the disciples broke the traditions of men by eating grain on the sabbath, but they zealously obeyed and fulfilled the "heart of the law which is mercy."

"The Son of Man is Lord—even of the sabbath." What bold claims Jesus makes, and what profound effects he has on our religion! In Jesus there is a greater than Jonah here, "and a greater than Solomon here." All law, all prophecy, and all wisdom are given by Jesus and should lead only to Jesus.

Finally, when the Jews tried to stand on their authority in Abraham, Jesus says, "I solemnly declare it: before Abraham came to be, I AM."

At that they tried to kill Jesus for claiming equality with God. In this Jesus declares that all things from God have only one purpose: to bring people to himself and to the good news of his "law" of love. All else is vain.

Are we sometimes scrupulous about the externals of our faith? Do judgments about these externals sometimes obscure our perception of our brother's and sister's true service of God and neighbor? Are we really people of the living Spirit, or people of a written law? Are the legal precepts we so scrupulously observe really the law of God, or are they mere traditions of man? Jesus must be the Lord of our own personal sabbath! Any renewal movement or new community in the church that does not have Jesus as its only Lord will lapse into vain, fruitless religion and will never minister life to the world. □

A Spiritual Counter Example
Luke 6:6-11 (23:Monday)

Is it lawful to do good on the sabbath—or evil? To preserve life—or destroy it? (v. 9)

Here Jesus cuts to the very heart of the question of religious law and tradition.

So often our laws and traditions start out doing good, but end by being so burdensome they actually prevent us from doing good. This often happens with church law. It can also happen with the laws and traditions of local communities. It happened with the Pharisees. They began as a reform group— a group to fight laxity and indifference. Among the chosen people to do so, they made laws dealing with every aspect of life, telling people about the right way to follow God. They added line upon line, and precept upon precept. What they ended with was a legal system so complex and externally demanding that it began to choke people's hearts and spirits so that no one could follow the heart and spirit of the law any more. As Jesus says of them, "You shut the doors of the Kingdom of God in men's faces, neither entering in yourselves nor admitting those who are trying to enter" (Mt 23:13). Do we do the same?

Jesus "knows our thoughts" and "looks around at us all" just like he did with the scribes and Pharisees. He challenges us to move beyond our human traditions and laws. He dares us to try and stop him as he opens the doors of the kingdom of God for the whole world. Then he reaches out fearlessly to heal a man with a withered hand.

Jesus tells the man to "get up and stand here in front." Jesus knew the thoughts of the Jewish leaders. He knew that he was upsetting their religious system of human tradition and laws, yet he acted boldly and without fear. He set a strong counter example of right against their wrong. We must now do the same. We must boldly and openly move beyond our mere external observances. Jesus stands the man he intends to heal up in front of them all.

We must be bold in setting a spiritual counter example, willing to bring this healing even when the scribes and Pharisees of our world are offended and plot to try and silence us. It is a matter of right and wrong. It is a matter of life and death. □

All Night in Prayer
Luke 6:12-19 (23:Tuesday)

Then he [Jesus] went out to the mountain to pray, spending the night in communion with God. At daybreak he called his disciples and selected twelve of them to be his apostles. (v. 12-13)

How many of us really prepare for the major choices and decisions of our life with such radical prayer? Jesus didn't just take a little time to pray. He spent all night in prayer!

Such watchings or vigils are not always peaceful, contemplative experiences. It takes work to stay up and follow the Spirit to the mountain. Yet the Spirit fills us with a fire that burns constantly in our hearts without yet consuming us. When God has called me to such all night prayer experiences, there is only one word I can use to describe it: "charged." I might be very tired, but I find my mind and my body charged with the energy of the Holy Spirit so that I am compelled to stay up and pray even as Paul was compelled by the Spirit to preach the gospel.

Usually my prayers are very directed, and I find inspiration and excitement from the Spirit as I pray. God speaks and I must listen! It is literally as if God shakes me from my sleep to talk to me about a particular decision I am about to make. Issues once unclear become clear as I listen to the Spirit. Darkness becomes light as the Spirit burns within my heart. I find this experience clarifying and inspiring. I believe Jesus had such an experience of prayer before making the important choice and life-changing decision about his twelve apostles.

Do we take the time for such prayer? Even when we are tired and weary, do we give place to the Spirit when God calls us aside to a special place to spend the night in prayer? Such prayer takes obedience and effort, but the grace received far exceeds the effort expended.

After prayer, Jesus then came down from the mountain to preach, heal and cure those with unclean spirits. People came from all around to hear Jesus, and to be touched by Jesus for "power went out from him which cured all."

If we want great things to happen in our life, we must make great effort to ascend the mountain and pray. Jesus also had to make an effort to descend the mountain back into the crowded world in order to work great miracles. We must make an intentional effort to follow the leading of the Spirit when we feel his promptings. We must allow ourselves to be compelled by God to do extraordinary things like spending the night in prayer, or going among the multitudes of the poor. Then, and only then, will the power of the Spirit go out from us to preach, to heal, and to cure the ills of this crowded world. □

Learn from the Poor
Luke 6:20-26 (23:Wednesday)

Then, raising his eyes to his disciples, he said: Blest are you. . . ." (v. 20)

Such words cut to the very heart and soul of our modern, western civilization. Jesus does not say "blessed are the poor in spirit" here. He says, "Blest are you poor" and "woe to you rich." Luke's version of the beatitudes is far more confronting than the versions found in the other gospels.

Our culture is extremely affluent. So much so that our wealth is not just a matter of God-given blessing, but also of greed. We are one-tenth of the world's population hoarding nine-tenths of the world's wealth. We go far beyond our legitimate needs, and spend most of our life pursuing our wants. We must realize that our wants can kill the needy.

The Letter of James speaks clearly to the rich of our nation saying, "Here, crying aloud, are the wages you withheld from the farm hands who harvested your fields. . . . You lived in wanton luxury on earth . . . you condemned, even killed the just man." How can some of our businesses continue to exploit poor laborers of other countries in the face of such words? How can we continue to live in luxury when the rest of the world starves?

Jesus says, "Woe to you rich; woe to you who are full; woe to you who laugh now." James says, "Begin to lament, to mourn, and to weep. Let your laughter be turned into mourning and your joy into sorrow." Such repentance will lead us to the greater blessing and joy of God. "Learn of the poor. Learn their ways, then you will learn of Christ. Learn of me for I am meek and lowly of heart," says the Lord. Let Jesus transubstantiate not only bread and wine. Let him transubstantiate the poor, so that he may continually come to us as he did on earth through them. Learn their sorrow and pain so that you may learn the blessing of Jesus' compassion. As Paul says, "Weep with those who weep, and rejoice with those who rejoice." He then "comforts us in all our afflictions and thus enables us to comfort those who are in trouble with the same consolation we have received from him." Then will you "put away ambitious thoughts," change your affluent, comfortable life-style and "associate with those who are lowly." Then will you become poor in spirit.

Here we can learn the blessedness of poverty. Becoming poor ourselves, we come to sensitively care for the poor, for we know their needs. Our heart is thus enriched by love in this poverty. Divesting ourselves of our illegitimate wants, we can give to the needy, saving their lives by meeting their legitimate needs. Our own spiritual life is now restored.

Are we willing to become the poor to save the poor? Are our hearts truly compassionate towards the needy? Do we really give up our wants to save the lives of the needy? These are questions Jesus calls us to answer today. If we cannot answer them, we cannot know the fullness of salvation which is "the good news preached to the poor." □

Let Your Heart Be Changed
Luke 6:27-38 (23:Thursday)

To you who hear me, I say: Love. . . . (v. 27)

Here Jesus begins to expound upon the "blessing" and "curses." If yesterday's "great discourse" could be likened to the ten commandments of the new covenant, today's teaching can be likened to the rest of the law. This section explains the "hard sayings" of yesterday's gospel.

But they still challenge us to radically change our behavior. Jesus says, "Love your enemies." Do good to those who try to do you wrong. Give a blessing to those who try to curse you. Pray for those who try to harm you. When someone steals from you, give them a little extra to make sure they have enough. What absurdity! He cuts to the heart of the whole system of acceptable behavior.

I believe Jesus wants us to do these things not simply to make a wrongdoer feel guilty. I believe he wants us to have a heartfelt love and concern for those who abuse or persecute us. "Be compassionate; do not judge; pardon." These are all heart realities. He cuts to our heart, so that our heart might be changed. He wants us to think of ourselves as the poor, who own nothing and, therefore, have no rights, no self-esteem, and no property to defend. "Esteem all others as better than ourselves," says Paul. We must "sell everything and give to the poor," if we are to fully follow Jesus. All we are called to do is love, and love all. This love cannot be free and from our heart as long as we possess anything but God in our hearts.

Jesus also tells us about giving to the poor. "Give to all who beg from you." It is not enough to lend to those from whom we expect to be repaid, either in money or in any other way. We can't always make their progress towards self-sufficiency a pre-condition for our generosity. To demand such progress as a result of our charity is, in the end, egotistical and self-exalting. Our ego wants to know it has had a positive effect on someone. "Even sinners lend to sinners, expecting to be repaid in full," says the Lord.

"Lend without expecting repayment. Then will your recompense be great. Then will you rightly be called sons of the Most High." We must quit trying to play God with the poor, and let God be God. To love while expecting repayment of any kind is egotistical and is, in effect, idolatry. All Jesus calls us to do is to believe in him, love from our hearts, and give. He will do the rest, for he is God.

Such "foolish" abandonment in loving and giving brings us joy. Such joy is a fruit of living in the Spirit. In the Spirit we will fulfill these teachings of Jesus with joy and perfect inner peace. Francis of Assisi is said to have experienced such perfect joy. Because he possessed nothing in his heart, he could give everything to the poor without worry. Because he sought only the cross of our Lord, he considered it joy when he was persecuted; plus he even loved his persecutors, for they helped him to draw closer to Jesus. Francis was joyful and free. Francis was a man of the Spirit. □

Do You Know Jesus?
Luke 6:39-42 (23:Friday)

Can a blind man act as guide to a blind man? (v. 39)

This is the teaching most central to a radical Christian lifestyle. If we want to change the world, we must first change ourselves!

The church is filled with movements and programs to

change the world. We have peace programs, social justice programs, evangelization programs—the list goes on and on, but none of these programs will effectively change the world if the hearts and lifestyles of the people in the programs are not first changed by Jesus. We cannot bring world peace unless we first know inner peace. Lasting peace comes only from Jesus and the Holy Spirit. We cannot bring justice, until we first know the justification given to us as a gift in Jesus through the forgiveness of our sins. We cannot evangelize until we have first been evangelized!

Otherwise we become simply the "blind leading the blind." We try to remove the speck in our brother's eye when there is still a plank lodged in our own eye. Jesus minces no words in calling those who do these things hypocrites.

As Christians we are not to be guilty of such personal hypocrisy or such cultural ineffectiveness. We are called to "be on a par with our teacher," Jesus. But even as Jesus spoke only what he first learned from the Father, we can speak only what we learn from Jesus. We are called first to go with Jesus into the desert ourselves to be tempted by the devil, so we might rightly help those in temptation. We are called to be fully born into humanity so that we might really help others in their human struggle. We are called to embrace the cross daily, so that we might help our brothers and sisters to bear the weight of their own daily crosses. Jesus "bore our sin and earned our sorrow" so he might save sinners and comfort the sorrowful. If we are to change the world with God's love, we must do the same.

Do we really know Jesus, or do we just talk about him? Do we really know his peace in our heart, or do we try to fill up the empty place in our hearts with programs, marches, and meetings? Such things without Christ will fail in the end, and will only be an idol in our own souls. Without Jesus there will be no peace, no justice, and no good news for the world. We must now seek only to sit at the feet of the Master as students, so we might rightly teach the whole world of truth. □

By Faith or by Works?
Luke 6:43-49 (23:Saturday)

*Each tree is known by its yield. . . . Why do you call me "Lord, Lord,"
and not put into practice what I teach you? Any man who desires to
come to me will hear my words and put them into practice.* (v. 44,
46-47)

Is salvation by faith or by works? Protestants say by faith,
while Catholics say by faith and by works. Perhaps Catholics
and Protestants do not properly understand what the other
group really teaches. Or perhaps we do not understand what
we ourselves teach. Is there a conflict? Scripture provides an
answer.

Paul says, "Salvation is yours through faith. This is not your
own doing, it is God's gift; neither is it a reward for anything
you have accomplished." Or simply, "We hold that a man is
justified by faith apart from observance of the law." Yet James
also says, "Faith that does nothing in practice is thoroughly
lifeless. . . . You must perceive that a person is justified by his
works and not by faith alone. . . . Be assured then, that faith
without works is as dead as a body without breath." Who is
right, Paul or James? Are they in conflict or in harmony? Are
the scriptures in harmony, or does this conflict annul their
credibility?

It is not a matter of comparing Paul to James. It is a matter of
comparing them both to the words of Jesus. Neither Paul nor
James is the cornerstone of our faith. Jesus is! Paul himself
says, "One of you will say, 'I belong to Paul,' another, 'I belong
to Apollos,' still another, 'Cephas has my allegiance,' and the
fourth, 'I belong to Christ.' Has Christ, then, been divided
into parts?" He says of such divisions, "If you go on biting and
tearing one another to pieces, take care! You will end up in
mutual destruction." The body of Christ is one. Paul and
James are united in Christ. Faith and works, likewise, become
one in Christ. If there is one, so must there be the other. Faith

without works is dead, but works without faith is vain. They will accomplish nothing.

Jesus says in today's gospel that a true desire for him will bring forth the fruit of faith in good works. If we really desire Christ, we will seek to follow him. If we do not follow him, we probably do not really desire him. Works become, therefore, a candid and stark measure of our desire and our faith. It is frightening but often true.

This desire then, is itself, a work of God's grace. It cannot be earned. But we must respond by acting on this desire. God holds out the gift of salvation to us, and he implants within us the desire for that gift. But if the desire is real, we will reach out through our actions to receive this gift of God. If we do not act, the desire is not really within us.

Do we act on the words of Jesus? Do we really desire to follow Christ, or do we hide behind a myriad of words and rationalizations rather than actively following Jesus? James says, "Do you believe that God is one? You are quite right. Even the demons believe, and shudder." It is not enough to talk the talk if you can't walk the walk. If all we do is talk, we are no different from the demons. ☐

Faith Means Love
Luke 7:1-10 (24:Monday)

I have never found so much faith among the Israelites. (v. 9)

The same Jesus who said his mission was first to the lost sheep of the house of Israel, and who at first would not give the food of God's table to the non-Jewish "dogs," here again commends the great faith of a Gentile, an outsider, a believer from another land. What was so special about the Roman centurion's faith?

Notice that his faith is manifested by his love for others. "He deserves this favor from you because he loves our people," say the Jewish elders who intercede to Jesus for him. This divine love has broken through the barrier of racial difference, and has built a bridge of human concern between two opposing peoples. His love is known to all and makes him "deserving" of Jesus' visit.

The centurion, however, is very humble about his faith. "I am not worthy to have you enter my house," he says to Jesus. He is great in the eyes of others, yet unworthy in his own eyes. Yet this does not hinder the radical boldness of his belief. "Just give the order and my servant will be cured." He is humble, yet bold in faith. Generous in love and humble in faith, he is seen by Jesus as greater than any Jewish believer he has encountered.

Are we willing to recognize the faith of other believers? They may not be from our tradition or our church, yet their love and their faith might far exceed the witness of the "chosen." Their great love and faith will justify them before God, yet so often we continue to judge and exclude them. This is not the attitude of Jesus with the Roman centurion.

Is our faith really made up of a humble love? Do we see ourselves as worthy or unworthy? Are we quick to justify ourselves, but quick to condemn others for their beliefs or practices? Better yet, does all the world see our faith through our love? Such divine love will break down the human barriers of race, creed, and political persuasion and build bonds of peace that unite us all in God.   □

Praise to Our God
Luke 7:11-17 (24:Tuesday)

A great prophet has risen among us . . . God has visited his people. (v. 16)

After Jesus healed the widow's son in the town of Naim, this was the cry of the people. "Fear seized them all and they began to praise God," says the gospel.

Do we really praise God for the miracles in our life, or do we soon forget them, or take them for granted? How many times God has visited us, and in how many wonderful ways! Yet we soon forget and fall back into our complacency.

"Remember" is a word frequently used in psalms and canticles of the Old Testament. We, too, must remember the great things God has done for us; the times he has visited our people. This remembrance will lead us to praise, and this attitude of praise will lead us to a life of joy!

"The dead man sat up and began to speak. Then Jesus gave him back to his mother." Notice that this healing unifies a family separated by death. How many times have we become dead to our family and friends through sin? We stop listening, or cease to simply take time to care. These attitudes are the first steps to killing a family relationship of openness, trust, and love. Jesus raises up the dead sons and daughters of our family, causes them to speak again, and restores us all to our mothers and fathers. Jesus can unite our broken families again.

Do we see Jesus as the great prophet who can speak God's healing word to us? Do we realize that when Jesus visits us that it is actually God visiting us through his Son? Let us turn this day to Jesus in order to be visited by God. Then we will be healed and our life will be a joyful life of praise! □

Be Hidden in Christ
Luke 7:31-35 (24:Wednesday)

We piped a tune but you did not dance. We sang you a dirge but you did not wail. (v. 32)

How similar this is to the words of Ezekiel the prophet: "For them you are only a ballad singer, with a pleasant voice and a clever touch. They listen to your words, but they will not obey them. But when it comes—and it is surely coming!—they shall know that there was a prophet among them."

How many times have I felt just this way after a concert.

Knowing that God's Spirit is calling heart after heart to himself, I find it frustrating to still be exalted by the crowd for my musical talent. Would that they could always see through my song to the Divine Singer.

Jesus must have experienced this frustration many times over. The crowds flocked to him because he worked miracles, yet they were unable to understand his real message.

In the end it would be that same crowd that flocked to his miracles and who greeted him upon his triumphal entry into Jerusalem who would cry out to crucify him. How painful it must have been to be so misunderstood.

Don't we do the same thing today? We flock to Jesus when he works miracles. We go to concerts, conventions and seminars. We support media ministries and evangelism rallies. But when it comes to the little things that go unnoticed by the world, we remain unexcited. It takes the power of the Spirit for us to help a shut-in or a street bum when nobody applauds. Very few will congratulate you for being faithful in marriage or building a quiet, but stable Christian family. It only takes our human ego to feel secure in supporting the popular gospel of the air waves. It takes the power of God to remain faithful with Jesus and Mary in Nazareth during the "silent years." We must be willing to do the small things before we can safely engage in the big. We must be willing to be hidden in Christ before he will manifest our work to the world.   □

Look to the Heart
Luke 7:36-50 (24:Thursday)

If this man were a prophet, he would know who and what sort of woman this is that touches him—that she is a sinner. (v. 39)

Do we look beyond the externals of morality, culture, and religion and look to the heart? Do we allow ourselves to be touched, kissed, even washed by the tears of sinners? Most of the time we do not. We confuse prophecy with judgment rather than an inner knowledge that looks to the heart, and judgment with condemnation rather than mercy and justice.

The Pharisees said of Jesus, "If this man were a prophet, he would know what sort of woman this is that touches him—that she is a sinner." Likewise, they provided no water to wash with, no kiss of greeting, and no perfumed oil of anointing for Jesus. Despite their rigorous religious exercises, they were sensitive neither to Jesus nor to a sincere repentant sinner.

The woman was a known sinner, yet she experienced a radical change of heart. From her repentant heart, tears flowed and fell upon the feet of Jesus. Where she once embraced and caressed men for profit, now she wipes Jesus' feet and anoints his head out of reverence. The external acts are made holy because of her change of heart.

Jesus responds, "I tell you, that is why her many sins are forgiven because of her great love. Little is forgiven the one whose love is small. . . . Your faith has been your salvation." Here Jesus directly connects faith and love.

It is not enough to be religious without having a heart of love. "God is love," says John. James reminds us that true religion consists of "looking after orphans and widows and keeping oneself unspotted from the world." How can one look after orphaned children and widowed women and mothers without having their hearts moved? The world tells us to look out for yourselves while James says we must not be defiled by this self-centeredness which hardens the human heart. "Love covers a multitude of sins," says the proverb. So today must we be people of human love if we are to profess true faith in God.

Today look to the sinner: the prostitute, the whore, the drug addict, and let your heart be moved. Treasure their tears, let them anoint your head. Let them kiss you and touch your life. Ironically, you might find your own life "cleansed" by the "unclean," and your openness may open the door to their salvation. Take a risk with Jesus. □

Grass Roots Ministry
Luke 8:1-3 (24:Friday)

Many others who were assisting them out of their means (v.3)

It is a little reassuring to know that even Jesus' ministry needed benefactors, or financial supporters. True, Jesus' ministry was carried out in poverty: "Take nothing for your journey," he instructed the twelve. He also told them, "Stay at whatever house you enter, eating and drinking what they have, for the laborer is worth his wage." Jesus and his disciples might have lived in poverty, but someone with at least some wealth had to give them food and shelter.

How different are our ministries today! Instead of living in gospel poverty and asking only for room and board to minister, our contemporary ministers stay in the finest hotels and eat in the finest restaurants. Instead of setting off on foot, we will travel only by jet, and then only first class! I cannot help but be reminded of Paul's words, "Such men value religion only as a means of personal gain. There is, of course, great gain in religion—provided one is content with sufficiency . . . if we have food and clothing, we have all that we need . . . the love of money is the root of all evil." Unfortunately, many of our modern, jet-set ministries seem to love money more than they love God.

The ministry of Jesus was more of a grass roots ministry. It had none of the show-biz hype that so often accompanies our concert "gospel star" syndrome. Jesus simply "journeyed through towns and villages preaching and proclaiming the good news of the kingdom of God." He taught, he healed, he delivered, and he called many to follow him. Soon the twelve were with him. Also other men and women followed him from town to town in a caravan of discipleship. It was a travelling community of faith, hope, and love that eventually changed the whole world.

This following developed because Jesus was willing to minister one-to-one, person-to-person. He taught in the little synagogues in the small villages and towns of Galilee. Only after this did he begin to minister in the open countryside to thousands. Only later did he go to Jerusalem to teach in the temple. Ironically, it was there that he was rejected.

We are called today to support the ministry of Jesus by accompanying the works and financially supporting the work. But what kind of ministry are we to support? Is it the big is better pattern of typical American evangelism, or is it the more grass roots ministry of Jesus? Is it a ministry that just ministers through mass media, or is it a ministry that takes time for the one-on-one, person-to-person approach? Is it a ministry that is willing to go forth in gospel poverty, or is it made up of ministers who live in luxury and wealth? These are all valid questions.

As for ourselves: are we willing to give more than just money to a ministry? Are we willing to accompany Jesus and his ministers as they preach and heal? Will we donate a day, a week, a month, or even a year to go to the mission field ourselves to preach the good news to the poor? Are we willing, not only to financially support a work, but actually to roll up our sleeves and do some of the hard work ourselves? Jesus doesn't want our money. He wants our life, our time; he wants our very soul. □

Hold on to the Gospel
Luke 8:4-15 (24:Saturday)

A farmer went out to sow some seed. . . . The seed is the word of God. (v. 5, 11)

"Those on the footpath are people who hear, but the devil comes in and takes the word out of their hearts lest they believe and be saved." How does the devil come? Will he steal the seed of God's word even before it has a chance to take root and grow in the soil of our life and soul?

Peter's First Letter says, "Stay sober and alert. Your

opponent the devil is prowling like a roaring lion looking for someone to devour." Paul says, "My fear is that, just as the serpent seduced Eve by his cunning, your thoughts may be corrupted and you may fall away from your sincere and complete devotion to Christ. I say this because, when someone comes preaching another Jesus than the one we preached, or when you receive a different spirit than the one you have received, or a gospel other than the gospel you accepted, you seem to endure it quite well . . . such men are false apostles. They practice deceit in their disguise as apostles of Christ."

It is not good to be overly conservative, for as John Henry Newman said, many of the early church heresies came from people so conservative that they could not accept the continuing development of the word of God within the church. Even as the water of a river takes on different appearances as it meets the various obstacles in its path, so does a doctrine take on different developments as it meets more specific questions during the life of the church. A tree looks radically different in its old age than it did in its youth. So too does a doctrine often sound different in its developed maturity than it did when it was still primitive and new. Many conservatives would keep the trees from growing, or the rivers from flowing in order to conserve only one dimension of God's truth. Such conservatism brings death.

But Paul tells us to faithfully conserve the gospel as we received it from the apostles. Some liberals today would place our scientific and psychological enlightenment above the revelation of Christ. Even as Eve tasted the forbidden fruit of the knowledge of good and evil, so do many Christians continue in this original sin by making the truth of God relative to the science of man. Some have even proposed Eve as the patron saint of the liberal church. They would say that Jesus not only spoke the cultural language of his day, but that he could not rise above the cultural understanding of his day. Of course, we have a better understanding today, even better than Jesus! Such people make Jesus' revelation relative to human science, rather than human science relative to God's revelation. This lowers the authority of God to the speculation of men and women, and leaves the human race lost in emotional and intellectual despair. They speculate about a Jesus they do not know and humanly rationalize about a divine power they do not understand. This speculation leads to relativism, and this relativism leads to both spiritual and moral despair. They try to destroy the authority of Jesus which "left the crowds spellbound," and cannot themselves rise to an authority any greater than that of the scribes who taught the Jews.

If we would seek to mystically know the real Jesus conserved in the teaching of the apostles, then our speculation would become real theology, real study of God. It would carry real authority. It would truly save!

The teaching of the church still carries this authority. Built "on the foundation of the apostles and the prophets, with Christ Jesus as the capstone," the church faithfully conserves the gospel as taught by Paul. At the same time, the church looks for ways to speak that word of God with authority in order to meet the challenges of the present day. More than any other institution on earth, the church stands up for the poor, for justice and peace, for human rights. More than any liberal political party or social activist group, the church speaks liberally about love while faithfully conserving the gospel of Jesus Christ. If we are conservatives with the gospel we will be liberals with the love of Jesus. If we are conservative with the love of the gospel we will destroy the very authority of the word of Jesus' love—and the foundation of Jesus' church.

Do we let the devil steal the word of God away from us? Do those who advocate justice and peace also advocate "another gospel" or a "different Spirit," or even "another Jesus" than that faithfully proclaimed throughout the ages by the church? Do those who advocate social justice really live in obedience to the greatest advocate of justice on the face of the earth—the church of Jesus Christ? Let us test the spirits as John tells us to.

With Timothy let us remain faithful to the scriptures and to the teaching of the apostles, for we "know who your teachers were." Then will the seed of the word of God have a chance to root deeply in the soil of our life and grow into a mighty tree. This tree will bear the fruit of the Spirit of God and will truly feed a hungry world. □

Give Your Gifts to Jesus
Luke 8:16-18 (25:Monday)

No one lights a lamp and puts it under a bushel basket or under a bed. (v. 16)

Do we use the gifts God has given us, or do we put our lamps "under a bushel basket"? Talents and gifts are like muscles: If we do not use them they will grow weak and disappear. If we use them they will grow strong and increase. We must use our gifts from God or he will take them away.

But we must also take our natural gifts to the foot of the cross if they are to be truly resurrected in Christ. Take my music for example: I was trained in the field of bluegrass and folk-country-rock. I had to completely let go of my music before God could raise up a totally new kind of sacred music through me. I died with Christ to folk-country-rock, and God raised up folk-classical-worship.

God will totally surprise us by raising up something far beyond our training or our wildest dreams if we will first die to our gifts and talents. What God gives will make us use our natural training, but will far surpass it with a supernatural surprise! Often our natural training will hold our gifts earthbound, while if we let go of our gifts, God will raise them into the heavens to soar on the wings of the Spirit. We must "let go and let God," or else our natural gifts will not really increase. Our spiritual muscles will not be used.

"There is nothing concealed that will not be known and brought to light." Are we willing to bring all of our natural gifts and talents to the supernatural light of Jesus Christ? Are we willing to let our natural gifts be "baptized so they might be raised up in new and exciting ways"? "Through baptism into his death we were buried with him, so that just as Christ was raised from the dead by the glory of the Father, we too might live a new life." Let us now use our gifts only for Jesus, so they might reach the full potential for which they were given to us by the Creator of the universe. Let us bring all our gifts to Jesus crucified, so they all might be given new life. □

Acting on God's Word
Luke 8:19-21 (25:Tuesday)

My mother and my brothers are those who hear the word of God and act upon it. (v. 21)

Do we just listen to the word of God, or do we really allow God to transform our entire life? It is one thing to study scripture and quite another to really become one of Jesus' disciples.

Acting upon God's word can be a frightening experience. It implies change. We are often called to reassess old habits and life-styles in the new light of Jesus' words. Sometimes these old habits and patterns are quite comfortable. We have grown accustomed to them, and it is risky business to change. It takes courage and faith.

It is like being tucked comfortably under our covers on a brisk fall morning. We have slept well and warm. The alarm rings, but the room is chilly and cold. All our inclinations are to simply remain under the covers and not get out of bed. But we know there is work to be done, so we make the decision to brave the cold and get up. So it is with acting on God's word. It is often our natural inclination not to change our old lifestyle. We must make a choice to follow Jesus in our actions as well as our words.

Consider the young bird who must use its wings for the first time. It does not even know it can fly until it is pushed from its nest. Similarly, we must jump into the thin air of faith before we can discover our spiritual wings. Once we find them, our life will never be the same.

How can we change our life today? Where have we grown comfortable and lukewarm, even at the expense of the destitute and the poor? We must grow hot for Christ, so we can bring heat to those dying in the cold. We must sacrifice our comfort, so others might have at least what they need to survive. Our life must change, or we cannot claim to be a part of the real family of Christ. □

Humble Ministry
Luke 9:1-6 (25:Wednesday)

Take nothing for your journey. (v.3)

How different is the ministry of Jesus from the mass media ministries of pop-Christianity! Instead of staying in first-class hotels, the apostles are to stay in the humble homes of the faithful. Instead of packing a wardrobe of the finest fashion, they are to take only the clothes on their backs. Instead of being dependent on truck loads of special equipment and staging gear, they are to "take nothing for their journey." The ministry of Jesus is simple and poor.

More than anything, the ministry seems grass-roots and personal. They stay in people's homes, rather than impersonal hotels. They not only preach, they reach out to heal the afflicted. They slowly travel on foot from village to village, rather than jetting across a nation in a few short days.

It is amazing to notice the difference between a walking ministry and a jet-set ministry. When I have set out on foot, I have had to slow down. Walking to a city gives you an entirely different perspective than flying into a city. When you walk, you must take the time to notice the individual homes, and the individuals within those homes. You notice the children in the yard, the flowers by the front steps, and the dogs or cats on the porch. You notice whether the homes are well kept or poor. You hear the music the people play. All these things bring you close to the people to whom you minister. I am not saying that media ministries and modern travel are wrong. I am saying it is wrong to lose the time to minister personally to people as human beings rather than as numbers in a ministry's computer.

Are our ministries personal or impersonal? Are we really concerned about the people to whom we minister, or are we just concerned about numbers and financial results? Are we willing to become poor for the sake of others, or do we seek to make a profit from our ministry? Jesus expects very clear answers to these questions from anyone who wishes to minister as his disciple, preaching and healing with his authority. □

Are You More Than Curious?
Luke 9:7-9 (25:Thursday)

[Herod] was very curious to see him. (v. 9)

Though Herod was curious about Jesus, he certainly was not one of Jesus' followers. For his part, Jesus does not seem too fond of Herod. He calls Herod "that fox" in response to the questions of his soldiers. Later, both Herod and his soldiers would treat Jesus with contempt before they sent him to be crucified by Pilate. Herod might have been curious about Jesus, but he certainly was not anxious to go beyond mere curiosity to real discipleship.

What about us? Are we only curious about Jesus? We might study for years about his life. We might be intrigued by his effect on cultural or even religious history. We might even be an ordained minister. But are we really anything more than curious? Are we really ready to radically change our life and become disciples?

A further question might be asked. Are people curious about us? Do we evoke the same response Jesus did, or does the world simply ignore us? If we are really his disciples, we should be evoking the same response that he did. Even our enemies should be curious about our ministries. If they are not at least curious, then we probably are not radical enough for Christ. If we have no enemies at all, then we probably have not stood up for anything at all!

Jesus stood up for truth. He spoke for God. He was a light in the darkness. Because of this he made enemies of those who wanted to remain comfortably in the darkness. Because his enemies were aware of his power, they were curious about him. The entire world should be curious about the activity of Christians, because Christians should be more than just curious about Jesus: They must be his disciples. □

Which Will You Choose?
Luke 9:18-22 (25:Friday)

Who do you say that I am? (v.20)

So it is with Christian life. We must daily answer the question: "Who do you say that I am?" It is not enough to answer the question once and then proceed as usual. No! We must answer the question every day as we face each challenge that lies before us.

Every day we have a choice. Will we acknowledge Jesus as the Christ of our life, or will we serve someone or something else? The choices are clear: peace or war, justice or injustice, love or hatred, light or darkness. With each person and circumstance we face today, we will have to make that choice.

The writer of the second-century Christian work *The Didache* speaks of the same choices. There lies before us the way of death or the way of life. Nothing much has changed in 1900 years. The Book of Sirach also says, "There are set before you fire and water. To whichever you choose, stretch out your hand. Before man are life and death, whichever he chooses shall be given him." The way of Jesus leads to life, and the way of self leads to death. Today we must choose between the two.

The way of Jesus seems to bring death, but it really brings life. We die to the world, but rise with him to eternal life in heaven. "Be intent on things above rather than on things of earth. After all, you died. Your life is hidden now with Christ in God," says the apostle Paul. We become poor by renouncing possessions, but we become rich in our newfound freedom from materialism. We become nobodies by renouncing the eminence of our positions, but we find the honor of associating with God's saints. We die totally to ourself, but we finally find ourself in a life serving others in God's love. This way leads to the cross of Jesus. But it is in the cross that we find a new way of life which lasts throughout eternity.   □

Death to Selfishness and Sin
Luke 9:43-45 (25:Saturday)

They failed, however, to understand this warning; its meaning was so concealed from them they did not grasp it at all. (v. 45)

So it is said in today's gospel concerning the disciples' response to Jesus' second prediction of his passion and death. They could understand his miracles. They could understand the traditional Jewish concept of a conquering Messiah. But the idea of a Messiah who would be killed was totally foreign to them. It seemed like complete defeat.

After Pentecost, however, their eyes would be opened. With the outpouring of the Spirit, they would come "to understand fully the mystery, the plan he was pleased to decree in Christ . . . to reconcile everything in his person both on earth and in the heavens, making peace through the blood of his cross." With the Spirit they could see beyond the externals of life and religion, and see into the very heart of God. This heart is a heart of love, so it is a heart of mystery. It lives by dying for those it loves. It is glorified in being humbled for those it loves. It is given abundant wealth by becoming poor so that those it loves might share in its wealth. These things are all paradoxes. They are all mystery. Yet they all boldly and clearly proclaim the truth of God's love. This love was most clearly revealed in the death of God's Son, Jesus the Christ.

Do we understand this mystery, or do we still seek a Messiah who will come in pragmatic, worldly victory? Do we really seek the action of the Spirit in our life so we might understand this mystery? Do we really allow ourselves to be daily born again in his love by coming to share in a daily death to selfishness and sin? As a post-pentecostal church, we must not allow ourselves to remain in the ignorance of the pre-pentecost disciples and followers. We must be born again. □

Do Not Discriminate
Luke 9:46-50 (26:Monday)

Whoever welcomes this little child on my account welcomes me. (v. 48)

Do we welcome the least of our brothers and sisters even as we would the greatest? James urges us in the second chapter of his letter to welcome "a poor man in shabby clothes" in the same way we welcome the influential and the rich. "Did not God choose those who are poor in the eyes of the world to be rich in faith and heirs of the kingdom he promised to those who love him? Yet you treated this poor man shamefully." We must not "discriminate in our hearts." We must welcome all as our brothers and sisters equally, like children of God.

Francis of Assisi welcomed all newcomers to his community in this way. He had an implicit trust in what the Spirit of God was accomplishing within those who were attracted to imitate his lifestyle. Moreover, he said he would obey a novice (of even one hour) gladly, if that novice were appointed to leadership! Francis welcomed all as children of

God so that he himself might remain a child before God.

We must have the heart of a child before we can welcome all people as God's children. *The Imitation of Christ* says, "Those who are evil within see all the world without as evil. But those who are pure within see all the world without them as pure." It is often those who are most sinful who are most skeptical of others, while those who are truly righteous trust others. "There is no limit to love's trust," says Paul. If we do not trust, it is often because we have not yet learned to love.

Do we really trust what the Spirit is accomplishing through our brothers and sisters? Do we really see the childlike followers of Jesus as those who know God's wisdom, or are we still judging by the standards of the world? Have we really nurtured a childlike purity within ourselves? If we have, then perhaps we are learning about God's love.   □

What If They Reject You?
Luke 9:51-56 (26:Tuesday)

The Samaritans would not welcome him because he was on his way to Jerusalem. (v. 53)

Yesterday's reading warned us not to stop those of another gospel "company" because "any man who is not against you is on your side." It warns us to be ecumenical and accept those of other Christian expressions, even if we cannot join them.

Today's reading asks us how we respond when we are, ourselves, rejected by other believers. The Samaritans accepted only the five books of Moses, or the Torah. They rejected all the prophets, the psalms, and the wisdom books as uninspired additions to the scripture. Because of this they did not worship at the temple in Jerusalem, the City of David. They also rejected all Jews who accepted the ongoing revelation of God through the traditions and writings of God's people.

Catholics are often similarly rejected by certain fundamentalist groups. We accept the scriptures plus God's ongoing revelation through the traditions and extra-biblical writings of God's saints. Because of this we celebrate the eucharist and have a rich sacramental and devotional heritage which brings us close to the Spirit and truth of Jesus. Some Christians reject us because we accept Jesus in these ways.

How do we deal with this rejection? Do we, like the disciples, ask Jesus to "call fire from heaven and destroy them," or do we retain our pace and simply "set off for another town"? Jesus tells his apostles, "When people will not receive you, leave that town and shake its dust from your feet as a testimony against them." He leaves all judgment until the day of judgment. Until then, Jesus walks the path of peace with his enemies, even when it cost him his life. Do we walk this path of peace even with other Christian faiths who reject us? Are we willing to lay down our life and the pride of being of the apostolic tradition or "company" in the pursuit of peace and unity with other Christians?

True, we must sometimes judge matters of faith and morality within the church. We should not give up our apostolic authority, only the *pride* of it. "Is it not those inside the community you must judge," asks Paul. Yet, he also says, "God will judge the others. . . . If possible live peaceably with everyone. Beloved, do not avenge yourselves: leave that to God's wrath." Let us not try to avenge ourselves. God will defend our position. □

Never Look Back
Luke 9:57-62 (26:Wednesday)

Whoever puts his hand to the plow but keeps looking back is unfit for the reign of God. (v.62)

We are here reminded of the story of the destruction of Sodom and Gomorrah. The angels told Lot, "Flee for your life! Don't look back or stop anywhere on the plain." But as they were leaving the city, Lot's wife looked back, and she was turned into a pillar of salt.

In the book of Revelation we are told concerning Babylon the Great: "Depart from her, my people, for fear of sinning with her and sharing the plagues inflicted on her." What is this city, "Babylon the Great"? Is she not any society or culture which compromises or prostitutes itself for earthly gain? "Come, I will show you the judgment in store for the great harlot who sits by the waters of the deep. The kings of the earth have committed fornication with her, and the earth's inhabitants have grown drunk on the wine of her lewdness."

We must come out from such materialism and lewdness. Our present culture is overwhelmed with these two things. We are bombarded with them at every turn. Television, radio, and magazines and newspapers are filled with these two things. We are constantly programmed with information that says it is normal to be both rich and sexually promiscuous, when in fact it is not. It has only become normal because we believed this lie.

We must not only come out of this culture, we must not look back. But how can we help looking back when we are constantly surrounded by it? The answer is simple: control the company you keep. Likewise, discipline your television and radio habits. Only read things that are wholesome and edifying. Paul says of speech, "Say only the good things man really needs to hear." We could easily apply this saying to the media: "Listen to, watch, and read only the good things men really need to hear." Paul says, "Bring your thoughts into captivity" and "Make no provision for the desires of the flesh." You cannot do this if you do not discipline your use of the media.

If you do not limit your use of the media, you will find yourself looking back lustfully at everything you were supposed to have left behind. The same holds true for the company you keep and the friends you associate with. "Bad company corrupts good morals," say the scriptures. If you keep looking back, you will eventually turn back and be destroyed in the fire of lust, materialism, and all other kinds of sin.

Do you secretly desire to go back to the life you left behind? Do you sometimes look back? Stop, or you will destroy any progress you have made in Christ thus far. Then you will have to start all over again, and someday it might be too late to begin again. □

Working for Christ
Luke 10:1-12 (26:Thursday)

The Lord appointed a further seventy-two and sent them in pairs before him to every town and place he intended to visit. (v. 1)

Jesus sent out the seventy-two disciples "in pairs before him to every town and place he intended to visit." As he gathered more and more followers he began involving them in his ministry, so that they would not only receive from him, but give to others what he had given to them. Jesus formed a travelling community of prayer and ministry.

Jesus sends them out in poverty. The less they have with them, the more unencumbered they will be to minister. "No soldier becomes entangled in the affairs of civilian life ... if we have food and clothing we have all that we need," writes Paul to Timothy in obedience to the words of Jesus. Jesus gives his disciples practical advice about ministerial "life on the road." He wants them to be free to devote themselves wholly to God and to ministry.

He sends them out "as lambs in the midst of wolves." They are to be examples, the "little ones" who do great things for God. They are not to be proud or pretentious, relying on their own strength or talent to preach the gospel. Their poverty is a prophetic sign of their complete dependence on God's providence. They are to receive whatever hospitality is offered them.

Yet they are not without boldness. They go forth in the authority of Jesus, who himself goes forth in the authority of his heavenly Father. If they are not welcomed in a town, they are to let the people know in no uncertain terms that they have rejected the reign of God. If a town rejects the disciples of Jesus "the fate of Sodom will be less severe than that of such a town." These are bold realities.

Are we willing to be bold in following Jesus? Are we willing to "prepare the way of the Lord"? Or are we so entangled in the materialism of this world that we simply don't have time for Jesus and his ministry? "The harvest is rich but the workers are few," says the Lord. Are you willing to sell all you possess and become a worker for Christ?   □

Can We Submit to the Church?
Luke 10:13-16 (26:Friday)

He who hears you, hears me. He who rejects you, rejects me. And he who rejects me, rejects him who sent me. (v. 16)

Jesus sends his disciples into the world to prepare the way for his coming. They are to announce that the reign of God is at hand. Jesus will then come to work the miracle of salvation.

Paul tells us, "Everyone who calls on the name of the Lord will be saved. But how shall they call on him in whom they have not believed? And how can they believe unless they have heard of him? And how can they hear unless there is someone to preach? And how can men preach unless they are sent?"

Jesus sends us out to preach the good news. Paul says, "I assure you, brothers, the gospel I proclaimed to you is no mere human invention. I did not receive it from any man, nor was I schooled in it. It came by revelation from Jesus Christ." So, too, were many of the prophets called and commissioned to proclaim God's word, without any human ordination or approval.

Yet Paul did eventually submit his ministry to the apostles in

Jerusalem. "I went prompted by a revelation, and I laid out for their scrutiny the gospel as I present it to the Gentiles—all this in private conference with the leaders, to make sure the course I was pursuing, or had pursued, was not useless." Even Paul, who was not afraid to disagree with Peter "because he was clearly in the wrong," submitted to his apostolic authority so much so that he said, "If anyone preaches a gospel to you other than the one you received, let a curse be upon him!" Strong words by a strong man who experienced the strength of apostolic authority because he first submitted in meek and humble obedience.

Jesus did not neglect to appoint leaders on earth while he was still on earth. This left a traceable, established line of authority. Today's gospel is taken from his instructions to those he personally appointed. Similar words were spoken to the Twelve. Because of the established line of succession from Jesus, Paul also appoints elders, or bishops, in every place where he founded a church. All the apostles did the same. From this the leadership of the early church claimed not only the prophetic authority of the Spirit, but the apostolic authority of Jesus as well.

Do we understand the harmony between the authority of the Spirit and the authority of the church today? Do we see our commission by Christ to evangelize as a ministry inside or outside the church? We must have the courage of a lone prophet and the humility of a submitted apostle if we are to truly evangelize the message of Jesus Christ today. We must sometimes call the church to repentance, but we must submit to her as well.

This is a great mystery and can only be understood by faith. Even as it takes the gift of faith to see the glory of Jesus within a humble portion of bread and wine, so does it take great faith to see the authority of Jesus infallibly transmitted through a church made up of weak and fallible people. This is a great miracle: the fact that the church still stands after two thousand years of assault and abuse from within and without is a miracle in itself. Any natural power or nation would have fallen long ago. Do we believe that Christ has worked this miracle called the church? Can we submit to her as unto the Lord? She is the bride of Jesus. She and he are one. If we do not submit to the bride, we reject the Groom as well. ☐

Great Miracles through Love
Luke 10:17-24 (26:Saturday)

What you have hidden from the learned and the clever you have revealed to the merest children. (v. 21)

How little our study and scholarship will accomplish without the gift of the Spirit, who supernaturally teaches us the truths of God. God the Father actually hides his truth from the proud scholar, while he chooses to reveal mystical secrets of heaven to the humble children. And this is the difference: "Knowledge inflates, love upbuilds."

Because of this humble and childlike faith the disciples did great things in Jesus' name. "Master, even the demons are subject to us in your name," they exclaim. He told them to cure the sick and to preach—and they took him at his word. Jesus said it, they believed it, and that settled it. Because of this simple acceptance of Jesus' words, great miracles were worked through simple men of humble upbringing.

But Jesus warns them not to rejoice that they worked miracles, but to rejoice because their names were written in heaven. It is not enough to work miracles in Jesus' name. We must know him so intimately that we develop a personal love relationship with him. Because he is in heaven, so will we now go to be with our lover and our friend. "In my Father's house are many dwelling places. I am going to prepare a place for you, and then I shall come back to take you with me, that where I am you also may be."

Do we really know Jesus? Is our knowledge of Jesus just a lot of religious information, or is it personal and loving, bringing salvation to the dark corners of our lives? Do we take him at his word, or do we muddy the clear waters of the gospel with our human rationalizations and idolatrous pride? If we want to evangelize for Jesus, we must first know Jesus. If we want to do miracles in his name, we must first receive him as a child. □

Live Radically
Luke 10:25-37 (27:Monday)

And who is my neighbor? (v. 29)

By his question, the lawyer was attempting to rationalize the radical nature of Jesus' words. Not content simply to hear, repent and obey, he was trying to take the edge off of Jesus' words so that he wouldn't really have to change his current and comfortable "religious" lifestyle.

We do the same thing today. We hear Jesus challenge us to change our lives radically. This makes us uncomfortable, but we aren't really atheist or agnostic people either. By and large we agree that we should believe in God.

We go to Bible studies and seminaries where we are told not only what Jesus said, but what he meant to say! Usually the interpretation is far less radical and challenging than the literal words of Christ. We would often rather meditate on a modern Bible commentary than on the Bible itself. We have conformed Jesus to our desired image rather than allowed the Spirit and his words to transform us into the image of Christ. Is this anything short of idolatry?

Notice that the people who come by the man who had been assaulted by robbers were all religious and respectable. Yet none of them did the will of God. It was a Samaritan, a fundamentalist heretic in the eyes of the Jews, who did God's will.

This was not so much a matter of worship or doctrine. It was a matter of the heart. Doctrinally, the Jews were correct, but they still did not please God. Doctrinally, the Samaritans did not perceive the full and ongoing revelation of God to his people through the prophets, the psalms, and the wisdom literature. Yet the Samaritan did the will of God because he had compassion.

Do we have compassion, or do we just have doctrine? Do we intellectually rationalize, or do we radically obey? Jesus wants disciples who allow their lives to be radically transformed by compassion and love. Without this our doctrines might be correct, but our life with God will still be wrong □

Spending Time with Jesus
Luke 10:38-42 (27:Tuesday)

Mary has chosen the better portion and she shall not be deprived of it. (v. 42)

So often we deprive ourselves of quiet time with Jesus and then try to deprive others of it as well. "A waste of time," we say. Or, "My work is my prayer." Here Jesus dares to contradict us.

Mary "seated herself at the Lord's feet and listened to his words." She does no work, even though there is work to be done. She leaves others to do the necessary tasks. She doesn't preach or evangelize. She doesn't feed the hungry, clothe the naked, or assist the poor. All she does is sit and listen to Jesus.

We are upset by this. We are much more comfortable with a spirituality which "baptizes" our hectic life of constant work for Jesus. We are "busy about many things." Entrepreneurs for Jesus . . . that's us! Always looking for opportunities to do big things for Jesus. Workaholics for Christ, we "lose ourselves" in work for the poor so that we will never have to face our own inner poverty. "Lord, are you not concerned that my sister has left me to do the household tasks alone? Tell her to help me." That's right, Jesus. Tell me you want and need all my work and effort.

Jesus answers us in gentle rebuke. "Martha, Martha, you are anxious and upset about many things; one thing only is required." Jesus does not require our work, our projects, or our evangelistic zeal. He requires only our love of him. We have only to sit at his feet and listen to him to meet the requirements of Christ. A heart of devotion and love pleases him more than a life of constant distraction in his name.

Do we spend quality time with Christ? If we would set aside undistracted time to be alone with an earthly lover, shouldn't we do all the more for our Divine Lover? He wants a personal love relationship that is unhurried and intimate, not a corporate agreement or work contract that is more fitting for a business relationship. Take time with Jesus today and you will end up taking better time with others.   ☐

Be Humble in Prayer
Luke 11:1-4 (27:Wednesday)

Lord, teach us to pray, as John taught his disciples. (v. 1)

Jesus teaches us not only that we should pray, but how we should pray. It is one thing to say that "Mary has chosen the better portion." It is quite another to respond to the sincere request, "Lord, teach us how to pray."

Jesus does not respond with some intricate method of mind or breath control. He does not write a book and travel the world giving seminars. He responds with a simple and short prayer. Yet this simple prayer covers all aspects of prayer and spiritual life.

First, there is praise, "Hallowed be your name." As the psalmist says, "Enter his courts with songs of praise, O Father, Lord of heaven and earth." Here is the heart of both active and contemplative prayer. It is the key to a new and a spiritually happy life, to "blessedness."

There is poverty of spirit and petition: "Give us this day our daily bread." Simple realization of our total dependence on

God for our whole life. "In him we move and breathe and have our being." Or, "In him everything in heaven and on earth was created, things visible and invisible. . . . In him everything continues in being." Without him we simply cease to be. We must come before him every day in poverty, making all people equal in the eyes of God.

"Forgive us our sins," teaches Jesus. Paul says, "For all have sinned and fallen short of the glory of God." Again, all must come equally before God. "There is neither Jew or Greek, slave or free, male or female." All races are equal, all classes, all cultures and ages! We are all equally poor, so we might equally be heirs to the riches of the kingdom! Mystical, yet practical.

"We forgive all who do us wrong," because we all "forgive as the Lord has forgiven you," to quote Paul. "He comforts us in all afflictions and thus enables us to comfort those who are in trouble with the same consolation we have received from him."

We sympathize and forgive because we are both guilty and forgiven. No one is better than another. All are poor and all are rich! "Subject us not to the trial." Again, Paul says, "He will not allow us to be tempted more than we are able to bear." We know Jesus was also tempted, "We do not have a high priest who is unable to sympathize with our weakness, but one who was tempted in every way that we are, yet never sinned." Jesus teaches us to pray, and truly understands the sincere prayers of us all.

Are our prayers humble, or are they pretentious? Do we take pride in our contemplation and charismatic gifts, or do we come in emptiness and poverty? Have we made a god out of prayer, or is our prayer simply a way to a personal relationship with God? Many pray, yet few really know God. Become poor and you will know God's riches. Be humble in prayer, and you will taste of his heavenly glory. □

Ask for the Spirit
Luke 11:5-13 (27:Thursday)

Ask and you shall receive; seek and you shall find; knock and it shall be opened to you. (v. 9)

Thus Jesus expounds on his teaching about prayer to his disciples. In Matthew's Gospel Jesus speaks about asking for "good things"; Luke here emphasizes asking for the Holy Spirit: "How much more will the heavenly Father give the Holy Spirit to those who ask him."

We are to ask for the Holy Spirit and good spiritual gifts of the Father if we are to be like trusting children before God. "Set your hearts on spiritual gifts," says Paul to the Corinthians. "Did you receive the Holy Spirit when you became believers?" he asks the disciples at Ephesus. So, too, with the desert father and the Russian Starets, the simple gift of the Spirit is seen as the pinnacle experience for the Christian mystic. Yet this gift is given to the smallest children in the kingdom.

We can ask for these things for the wrong reasons. Simon Magus even offered to pay Peter for it saying, "Give me that power too, so that if I place my hands on anyone he will receive the Holy Spirit." Peter responded, "May you and your money rot—thinking that God's gift can be bought!" Simon asked for the right thing for all the wrong reasons. Pride motivated him.

The same holds true for the "good things" we truly need. James says, "You ask and you do not receive because you ask wrongly, with a view to squandering what you receive on your pleasures." Yet even James begins his letter by emphasizing asking first for wisdom, "an aura of the might of God and a pure effusion of the glory of the Almighty." He says, "If any of you is without wisdom, let him ask it from God who gives generously and ungrudgingly to all, and it will be given him. Yet he must ask in faith, never doubting." As Jesus says, if whoever has "no inner doubts, but believes that what he says will happen, he shall have it done for him."

Do we humbly ask for the power of the Spirit in our life? When we ask, do we really believe, or do we secretly harbor doubts and think our request won't happen? We must ask and truly "expect a miracle." Even though we might be very "unspiritual," "all things are possible with God." He can give us spiritual power. If we ask humbly for God's glory, it will be done. □

The Battle with Darkness
Luke 11:15-26 (27:Friday)

When an unclean spirit has gone out of a man . . . (v. 24)

Once we have taken the time to become "contemplative," do we think ourselves beyond battles with basic sin? Jesus says the unclean spirit "goes out and returns with seven other spirits far worse than itself." Jesus himself experienced this: "When the devil had finished all the tempting, he left him to await another opportunity." Jesus battled temptation throughout his life.

The basic battle with darkness and sin is a daily process. Every day we must rise to choose Jesus one hundred percent. We cannot be divided. "Every kingdom divided against itself is laid waste," says Jesus. The successful disciple must "take up his cross each day." The decision must be total. It must be daily.

The spirits Jesus cast out and spoke of were unclean and caused men to be mute. They kept people from reaching their full potential by silencing them and covering them with the foulness and dust of earth.

"When the unclean spirit has gone out of a man"—The spirits that Jesus cast out of people ministered darkness and uncleanness. They brought destructive forces into people's lives. "Jesus was casting out a devil which was mute, and when the devil was cast out the dumb man spoke." By bringing sin into our life, these devils silence our capacity to praise and glorify God. They keep us from reaching the full potential God intends for each of us. For it is only in positive praise and thanksgiving that we move from the destructive negativity of sin.

Paul is aware of this battle going on even within his own soul. "I see in my body's members another law at war with the law of my mind . . . I do not do what I want to do, but what I hate." Paul lists many of these oppressive and compulsive sins which limit us when he says, "Put to death whatever in your nature is rooted in earth; fornication, uncleanness, passion, evil desires, and that lust which is idolatry."

"These are the sins which provoke God's wrath. Your own conduct was once of this sort, when these sins were your very life. You must put all that aside now: all the anger and quick temper, the malice, the insults, the foul language. Stop lying to one another . . . all that is out of place. Instead give thanks."

We must turn from these destructive and dark forces in our life in order to be born again. Otherwise, they will eventually take us over and become "our very life." Again Paul says we all once were this way, "You gave allegiance to the present age and to the prince of the air, that spirit who is even now at work among the rebellious. All of us were once of their company." Yet even now, as followers of Christ, we must "fight the good fight" and not give in again to the spirit of darkness and the desires of the flesh.

"Every kingdom divided against itself is laid waste." We must totally turn from the darkness or we will fail. We must put the old man totally to death, or we will never be fully resurrected. The death must be permanent and daily. The death must be total.

Jesus says, "Whoever wishes to be my follower must deny his very self, take up his cross each day, and follow in my steps." If this exercise of turning away from sin and turning towards Jesus is not practiced daily, we will turn back to our sin in an even more devastating way than the way we began. The unclean spirit "goes out and returns with seven other spirits far worse than itself, who enter and dwell there. The result is that the last state of the man is worse than the first." Our turning must be daily. It must be constant. Otherwise, we will become entangled again. "Never grow weary of doing good."

Have we turned totally from the sins of our past, or do we still toy with them in our memory? Do we still enjoy the way of darkness in our mind while trying to follow the way of the light in our actions? If you do not "acquire a fresh, spiritual way of thinking" you will never overcome the darkness in your flesh. Jesus will cast it out, but you will invite it back and it will grow stronger. Do you choose to let Jesus cast out your devils by dying with Christ daily, or do you still let sin live in the secret corners of your soul? If you want to love what God loves, you must hate what God hates. You must hate sin and turn from it daily if you want to turn to God.

As James says, "Therefore, submit to God, resist the devil and he will take flight. Draw close to God, and he will draw close to you. Cleanse your hands, you sinners; purify your hearts, you backsliders. . . . Be humbled in the sight of the Lord and he will raise you on high." ☐

Living the Gospel
Luke 11:27-28 (27:Saturday)

Blest are they who hear the word of God and keep it. (v. 28)

It is not enough to talk about the gospel. We must live it! We cannot just hear the radical words of Christ. We must change our life and keep his words.

We love to go to seminars, conventions, and rallies to hear radical teaching about Jesus. We all applaud and sing, and celebrate emotional liturgies. Then we go home and continue on with business as usual. Jesus says we must keep his words, as well as hear them if we are to be "blest."

This makes perfect sense. To assent to something in your mind, and dissent with something in your lifestyle is a blatant contradiction that leads to eventual frustration. To be blest means to be happy. You cannot ever be happy if you are frustrated.

If there is a contradiction between our belief and our life, then we must change either our belief or our life in order to be happy. "You cannot serve two masters." Likewise, "the kingdom divided against itself is bound for ruin." If we believe in Jesus, our life must be consistent with his words. Otherwise, we are living a lie.

Is our life consistent with our belief? Do we only listen to Jesus, or do we really follow him by giving him our whole life? Jesus says, "I have come that you may have life and have it abundantly." Only by living our belief in Jesus will we be truly fulfilled. Only then will we end our frustration and be truly happy. Only in Christ will our life be truly blest.   □

Don't Depend on Signs and Wonders
Luke 11:29-32 (28:Monday)

This is an evil age. It seeks a sign. (v. 29)

Are we also "sign seekers"? Jesus says, "Blessed are those who believe and have never seen" when Thomas seeks a sign of the holes in the Lord's hands, feet, and side. Hebrews says, "Faith is confident assurance concerning what we hope for, and conviction about things we do not see." Yet, so often our faith languishes and grows cold if it is not bolstered by continuous signs and wonders.

We also know that God has given us miracles so we might believe strongly. The book of Hebrews says of the gospel of Jesus Christ, "God then gave witness to it by signs, miracles, varied acts of power, and distribution of the gifts of the Holy Spirit as he willed." Paul includes the charismatic signs in his list of valid ministries in the church when he says, "God has set up in the church—first apostles, second prophets, third teachers, then miracle workers, healers, assistants, administrators, and those who speak in tongues." For Paul, signs and wonders were given to strengthen the church's faith. As the Acts of the Apostles says, "A reverent fear overtook them all, for many wonders and signs were performed by the apostles." This prompted believers to live radically for Jesus.

God gives us signs and wonders, but he doesn't want us to depend on them. He gives them to us when we are weak, but a strong faith no longer needs them. We should seek the Giver of the gifts, rather than only the gifts without the Giver.

Do we ask for signs and wonders because we have little faith, or do we ask in order to bring God's love to others? Do we seek spiritual gifts in order to glorify ourselves, or to glorify God? Do we seek only the gifts, or do we seek the Giver of gifts? Let us search our hearts so that we do not subtly become an "evil generation" in our seeking of signs and wonders. □

A Matter of the Heart
Luke 11:37-41 (28:Tuesday)

The Pharisee was surprised that he [Jesus] had not first performed the absolutions prescribed before eating. (v. 38)

We, too, are often shocked when our guests do not follow our religious customs. We are shocked when the externals of our faith are not followed.

Jesus corrects us in the Pharisee, "You Pharisees! You cleanse the outside of cup and dish, but within you are filled with rapaciousness and evil. . . . But if you give what you have as alms, all will be wiped clean for you."

Often we are caught up in the expensive externals of religion, but our hearts do not really grieve for the poor. We collect expensive religious art and observe all the rituals of our faith with reverence, but if anyone dares to cross us or our scrupulous rules, we become vicious and evil. We reverence the relics of the saints, but are irreverent towards the saints living among us today.

The poor and the simple do not necessarily know the latest

theological trend, or collect classic pieces of religious art, but they often love God more deeply than the "Pharisee" trend of our day. They do not always know the correct protocol for entering a church or praying in a group, or giving thanks before a meal; yet they reverence God more than we do.

We do not really love the simple and the poor. Jesus says, "As often as you did it for one of my least brothers, you did it for me." Yet we do not really see the King of Kings transubstantiated in the uneducated and the poor.

It is really a matter of the heart. The new covenant is written on the heart. Our hearts of stone must be transformed into hearts of flesh. The hearts can easily be pierced. They bleed. So was Jesus' heart pierced on Calvary.

Does our elaborate religious ritual lead us to the heart of Jesus, or does it only serve to hide our hearts of stone? Do we hang on to our wealth in the name of Jesus, when Jesus commands us to give all that we have to the poor? If we let go of all our religious games and allow our hearts to be broken with the needs of others, we will be made clean. Our rituals are useless if they do not change our hearts. If our heart is cleansed, then we will find Jesus even within those who do not observe our religious customs, and we will become tolerant and respectful of their difference. □

The Perils of False Religion
Luke 11:42-46 (28:Wednesday)

Teacher, in speaking this way you insult us too. (v. 45)

So we could all easily respond to Jesus.

Even though we tithe and give to the poor, many times our heart remains lukewarm. Even though we read about humility, we often seek places of respect within the religious world. Our Christian life appears in perfect order on the surface, but deep inside there is confusion, selfishness, and fear.

Francis of Assisi speaks of this situation when he says, "There are many people who spend all their time at their prayers and other religious exercises, and mortify themselves by long fasts and so on; but if anyone says as much as a word that implies a reflection on their self-esteem or takes something from them, they are immediately up in arms and annoyed. These people are not really poor in spirit." Francis knew with Jesus that mere external holiness was no sure sign of interior conversion.

Jesus says, "You are like hidden tombs over which men walk unawares." Jesus likens this hidden darkness to death. We may be religious outside, but we may be dying inside.

Ironically, when we are in this living death, we often inflict it on those around us. "You lay impossible burdens on men, but will not lift a finger to lighten them." Not only do we fill our own life with external legalism and ritual in order to try and dispel the darkness within, we inflict it upon those around us, filling their life with the unnecessary guilt of our pseudo-religion. It cannot dispel our darkness, nor can it dispel theirs. It only builds guilt upon guilt into an obsessive and compulsive religion that ministers spiritual death rather than life.

Jesus gives us no wonderful answers in this reading. He only confronts and condemns the darkness. Perhaps all we should do is examine ourselves. Not an examination of externals, but of internals. Examine your heart. Is your heart in darkness? Is your ritual only a frantic and frightened attempt to ignore this inner darkness? Do we try to "evangelize" others through this ritual when through it we ourselves have yet to really experience the good news? We cannot share what we do not have. □

Move Forward in Christ
Luke 11:47-54 (28:Thursday)

I will send them prophets and apostles, and some of these they will persecute and kill. (v. 49)

Do we "persecute and kill" the prophets of our day? Oh no, we cannot actually kill them, but God knows we can persecute them. We kill them with words sharper than any military sword.

How dare our prophets challenge us! How dare our apostles shine the light into our comfortable darkness! Are we not good Christians? Don't we attend church frequently?

"This generation will have to give account for the blood of all the prophets—shed since the foundation of the world." In a sense we are all responsible for the death of all the apostles and prophets when we ignore, persecute, or kill those sent to us today. The same response which killed those of the past is still alive within us today, so we are responsible for them all. The generation of Jesus' day was responsible in a special way since they crucified the Son of God. Scripture has it that we "crucify him afresh" when we willfully turn from Jesus. If we transgress "one point of the law, we are guilty on all counts," says James. Likewise, if we kill the prophets of our own day through our attitudes or actions, we participate in the murder of them all.

The prophet, John the Baptist, speaks to this generation: "Do not begin saying to yourselves, 'Abraham is our father.' I tell you, God can raise up children of Abraham from these stones. Even now the axe is laid to the root of the tree. Every tree that is not fruitful will be cut down and thrown into the fire."

Do not become too confident by relying on the righteousness of those who established our church. "What I mean is that each one of you says, 'I belong to Paul,' or, 'I belong to Apollos,' or, 'I belong to Christ.'" The book of Sirach even says, "Of forgiveness be not overconfident, adding sin upon sin. Say not 'Great is his mercy; my many sins he will forgive.'"

All of this can be confused with proper spirituality in Christ and his church, but in reality it is only presumption and pride. Forgiveness is good. The saints are good. Jesus is good. But presumption about all these things is bad.

The apostles and prophets of our day call us to holiness and deep personal relationship with Jesus Christ. Often this means we must change. But change can be uncomfortable, so we resist it.

You cannot follow Jesus and stand still. His footsteps are always before us, leading us forward. "Whoever puts his hand to the plow, but keeps looking back, is unfit for the reign of God." His footsteps lead to the cross.

Are we willing to be constantly challenged and called forward by Jesus? Are we willing to die to the things in our life that drag us down and keep us from following the Lord freely? Do we really listen to the apostles and prophets he sends to our life and our church today, or do we simply ignore them? Jesus is alive, and so must his church be. This means we must ever be ready to change and move forward in Christ. □

Bless Your Persecutors
Luke 12:1-7 (28:Friday)

Do not be afraid of those who kill the body and can do no more. I will show you whom you ought to fear. Fear him who has power to cast into Gehenna after he has killed. (v. 4)

Are we afraid of persecution? Are we willing to compromise our faith in order to avoid the physical pain or discomfort of persecution?

I live in a part of the United States where only two percent of the population is Catholic. The Ku Klux Klan still exists in some towns. Blacks may pass through, but all the residents are white. Neo-Naziism still thrives in survivalist camps and communities tucked away in the mountains. As a Catholic Franciscan community, we have often spoken out publicly for our faith. Most everyone knows our position on basic human rights, peace and social justice, and the gospel values of Jesus Christ which so motivate the church in our country.

I have often wondered what I would do if some lonely night a group of vigilantes invaded the peace of our mountain hermitage and began destroying both property and life. How would I respond to seeing my brothers beaten and my sisters abused and raped? God forbid that this scene would ever become reality. But if it did, I can only hope I would respond according to the example of Jesus.

The scriptures promise that we will all suffer persecution of some kind in response to our living as faithful Christians. Paul says quite simply, "Anyone who wants to live a godly life in Christ Jesus can expect to be persecuted." Peter says, "Do not be surprised, beloved, that a trial by fire is occurring in your midst. It is to test you, but it should not catch you off guard. Rejoice instead, in the measure that you share Christ's sufferings. . . . Happy are you when you are insulted for the sake of Christ. . . . If anyone suffers for being a Christian, he ought not be ashamed. Let those who suffer as God's will requires continue in good deeds, and entrust their lives to a faithful Creator."

Jesus himself promises, "All will hate you because of me." He says knowingly, "When they persecute you in one town, flee to the next." He also describes our response: "Love your enemies, do good to those who hate you; bless those who curse you and pray for those who maltreat you." As Paul says, "Bless your persecutors; bless and do not curse. . . . If possible, live peaceably with everyone. Beloved, do not avenge yourselves: leave that to God's wrath, for it is written: 'Vengeance is mine; I will repay, says the Lord.' But if your enemy is hungry, feed him; if he is thirsty, give him something to drink; by doing good you will heap burning coals on his head. Do not be conquered by evil but conquer evil with good." Violence only brings violence. Retribution only brings retribution. "Those who live by the sword will die by the sword," says Jesus. James speaks to the unjust and persecuting rich and describes the response of the Christian: "You condemned, even killed the just man; he does not resist you."

Do I rejoice in persecution today? Do I respond with non-resisting love, or do I try to avenge injustice shown myself and others? The persecution might be as extreme and devil-like as terrorism and violence done by a vigilante group or an unjust government. It might be as subtle as resistance to good and just ideas in business or civil planning. It might even come from the "wolves in sheep's clothing," the false prophets and teachers within the church. But it is around us constantly if we dare to follow Jesus radically. How do we respond? Will we keep the faith or compromise? Will we love or will we hate? □

Standing up for Jesus
Luke 12:8-12 (28:Saturday)

I tell you, whoever acknowledges me before men—the Son of Man will acknowledge him before the angels of God. (v. 8)

It can often be difficult to acknowledge Jesus before others. The world seldom speaks of Christ, except to use his name in vain. Jesus is no longer found on the front page of popular magazines as he was during the days of the Jesus Movement. Today the world is preoccupied with the pragmatic realities of political power and money. Even the born again movement has largely degenerated into a political movement emphasizing military strength and economic prosperity.

It takes courage to stand up for the real Jesus of Bethlehem and Calvary, born in a shepherd's stable and crucified on a criminal's cross. It is not easy to stand up for the poor, or to give one's life for those treated unjustly by the political systems of the world.

We may feel at a loss when asked to explain the way of Jesus. How can we put into words a spiritual reality that is proclaimed everywhere? How can we put into limited words an infinite Living Word proclaimed throughout eternity? "Where is the wise man to be found? Where is the scribe? Where is the master of worldly argument? Has not God turned the wisdom of this world into folly?"

Paul continues, "I did not come proclaiming God's testimony with any particular eloquence or 'wisdom' . . . my message and my preaching had none of the persuasive force of 'wise' argumentation, but the convincing power of the Spirit." As Jesus tells us in today's gospel, "The Holy Spirit will teach you at that moment all that should be said."

We need not win an argument. We need only proclaim the simple message of Jesus. "The word of God will not return void," says Isaiah the prophet. Only speak in clear simplicity and confidence. Let the Spirit do the rest. You may not win the intellectual argument, but you will win the spiritual battle for the soul! As Socrates said, "Just because you win an argument does not mean you possess the truth."

Do we really rely on the power of the Spirit when we share about Jesus with others? Do we share in the Spirit, or simply argue with the mind? The Spirit leads to humility and gentleness, while the mind only leads to presumption and pride. Do not be afraid. God will use your simple testimony and your personal story to evangelize even the powerful of this world. □

Greed Will Sidetrack You
Luke 12:13-21 (29:Monday)

Avoid greed in all its forms. (v. 15)

What are the forms of greed? We can be greedy for material things, but we can also be greedy for pleasure and power. Francis of Assisi says, "A man takes leave of all that he possesses . . . when he gives himself up completely to obedience in the hands of his superior." Annoyance at being told what to do or criticized by someone else indicates that you do not yet possess gospel poverty. You are still greedy.

Greed and lust are really very closely related. If you are lustful and greedy, your rightful needs have gotten out of control and have begun to possess your life.

Paul speaks of a list of vices that control a person's life and ends with "that lust which is idolatry." He also speaks of the power of these vices to take over our whole being when he says, "When these sins were your very life." Lust and greed take over a person's whole life so that one is "possessed by possessions."

Yet, in taking over our life they are unable to give life. Jesus says, "A man may be wealthy, but his possessions do not guarantee him life." How many people do we know who are wealthy and powerful, people who partake of every pleasure available on earth, yet they are still frustrated? The more you have the more you want. Possessed by such greed you end in frustration, no matter how wealthy or powerful you are, or how many pleasures you enjoy.

Jesus says, "I came that you may have life and have it abundantly." He speaks of eternal life. This includes life on earth, but far exceeds it. Our present life is only a preparation for eternity. It is only a rehearsal before the concert. It is only a boot camp before the real battle. Greed and lust tie us to this present world and limit our perception of the eternal future. "You fool! This very night your life shall be required of you. To whom will all this piled-up wealth of yours go?"

When we die we will stand before God. Will we be prepared? Greed and lust sidetrack us from our final goal and the real purpose of this passing, present life. Will we find in the end that we have wasted our precious time on earth on un-important and foolish things? Or will we be truly prepared for mature existence in eternal life? Let us not stop the process of maturing by being greedy for possessing things that have little eternal value. □

Follow Him Immediately
Luke 12:35-38 (29:Tuesday)

Be like men awaiting their master's return from a wedding, so that when he arrives and knocks, you will open for him without delay. (v. 36)

Would we "open for him without delay," or would we first have to free ourselves of our many idle pursuits? These idle pursuits are the cares and anxieties which distract and delay us from actively pursuing full and final union with Jesus Christ.

Even during his earthly life Jesus evoked an immediate response from his serious followers. The gospel says that his first disciples "immediately abandoned their nets and became his followers," or "immediately they abandoned their boat and father to follow him." Even Matthew, the tax collector, a man entrenched in the life of economics and business, "got up and followed him" without hesitation! Jesus himself says to the many who want to follow him only after the affairs of a dead relative are in order, "Follow me, and let the dead bury the dead." Jesus demands a response to his call that is both total and immediate.

"Let your belts be fastened around your waists and your lamps be burning brightly." Are we always ready for Jesus to call us forward, or do we disrobe and put out the lamps for occasional spiritual sleep? "Awake, sleeper! If today you hear his voice, harden not your hearts," says the scripture. "Brothers, never grow weary of doing good," says Paul. We must be ready every day to respond to the radical call of Jesus in our life. If we are asleep, we will not hear the call.

"Should he happen to come at midnight or before sunrise." Do we take time for vigils and watchings? To stay up waiting for the Lord when all the world sleeps is a powerful experience, for it symbolizes the preferable attitude of our whole spiritual life. Are we awake and watching even while the world slumbers? Are we in the sunlight, even while the world slumbers in the darkness of sin? Better yet, do we make the effort to rise and "fan into full flame" our gift of the Spirit even when by nature we tend toward spiritual sleep and darkness? This requires both faith and effort. Finally, in this faith and effort, are we always ready to follow the radical call of Jesus on our life?   □

Make the Most of the Time
Luke 12:39-48 (29:Wednesday)

When much has been given a man, much will be required of him. (v. 48)

What do we do with the gifts and opportunities God has given us? We are responsible for them. We will have to give an account before God.

How well do we use the time we have in this life? Paul says, "Make the most of the present opportunity." Jesus warns in today's gospel, "If the servant says to himself, 'My master is taking his time about coming,' and begins to abuse the housemen and servant girls, to eat and drink and get drunk, that servant's master will come back on a day when he does not expect him, at a time he does not know. He will punish him severely and rank him among those undeserving of trust." Will Jesus trust us with the very kingdom of God when we do not even use our time to advantage here on earth?

How do we use material things? In this parable we are called stewards of the master's property. We do not own the things we use, God does! As Paul says, "Buyers should conduct themselves as though they owned nothing, and those who make use of the world as though they were not using it, for the world as we know it is passing away. I should like you to be free of all worries." Those who "abuse" and "eat and drink and get drunk" will become tied to the earth and will lose their way to God. Do we use our possessions as if Jesus might return at any moment to take us to the heavenly kingdom? Why become attached to the furniture in the "waiting room"? What is important is the person you wait to see—Jesus the Lord! ☐

The Fire of the Spirit
Luke 12:49-53 (29:Thursday)

I have come to light a fire on the earth. How I wish the blaze were ignited! (v. 49)

Is God a fire in our life?

On the feast of Pentecost the disciples gathered in the upper room to pray. The power of the Holy Spirit descended on them with the audible sound of a "strong, driving wind." "Tongues as of fire appeared, which parted and came to rest on each of them. All were filled with the Holy Spirit. They began to express themselves in foreign tongues and make bold proclamations as the Spirit prompted them."

Do we allow the gifts of the Spirit to operate in our life? Do we seek these gifts, or do we think they are only for others? Paul says, "Set your hearts on spiritual gifts." It is okay to seek the gifts of the Spirit as long as they lead us to the Giver of the gifts and build up the spiritual strength of the church.

Paul goes on, "Be rich in those that build up the church.... Thank God I speak in tongues more than any of you, but in the church I would rather say five intelligible words to instruct others than a thousand words in a tongue." But "Set your hearts on prophecy ... and do not forbid those who speak in tongues." It is okay. And it is okay for us!

If we experienced this fire in our life in the past, do we still today? Paul says to Timothy, "Fan into a full flame the gift you have received." This is an active description. It is not enough to sit back passively and wait for God to stir up his power in our life. We must actively seek God to maintain our relationship with him. He is a Lover whom we must actively pursue, in order to express our love for him!

Every day I pray in tongues for a long period of time. This wordless prayer or praise raises my spirit above the petty disturbances of my mind and brings my spirit to God. It frees me from every anxiety of life, and enables me to go back to face my problems, renewed in spirit and clear in mind.

This zeal, however, is not always understood. Those you think will understand often do not. Religious family and community members often accuse you of being a fanatic or crazy. "From now on, a household of five will be divided," says Jesus. It takes courage to follow Jesus with such fire!

Remember, they called the saints crazy before they called them holy. They killed many of the prophets before they canonized their writings. It will be no different today. Paul says, "Anyone who wants to live a godly life in Christ Jesus can expect to be persecuted."

Are we willing to face persecution so we might come closer to the face of Jesus? Are we willing to fan the flame every day, or do we expect God to do all the work in our relationship with him? Are we really open to the fire of the Holy Spirit in our life, or do we put limits on God?

Fire is also a purifying force in our life. It comes by way of trial and tribulation. But these trials should be seen as a blessing rather than a curse for the follower of Jesus.

This fire of trial strengthens our faith. Peter also says, "There is cause for rejoicing here. You may for a time have to suffer many trials: but this is so that your faith, which is more precious than the passing splendor of fire-tried gold, may by its genuineness lead to praise, glory and honor when Jesus Christ appears.... Rejoice with inexpressible joy touched with glory because you are achieving faith's goal, your salvation." For the follower of Jesus Christ all things "work together for the good," says Paul. Fire may bring some initial pain, but in the end it purifies.

The first letter of Peter also says, "Do not be surprised,

beloved, that a trial by fire is occuring in your midst. It is a test for you, but it should not catch you off guard. Rejoice instead, in the measure that you share Christ's sufferings."

If we love Jesus with the "living flame of love," we will ardently long to consummate our union with him at the cross. It is not enough to simply sit back and passively accept tribulation in light of our hope for eventual relief. It is valid, but it is incomplete. We must actually find joy in suffering because we long to be united with our Lover who was crucified to reach out to us in love!

So let both the inner fire of love and the external fire of tribulation and trial burn. They only bring us into union with our Lover.

The fire will come. It is a given. It cannot be escaped. It will either come from within or without, in the present, or in the future, but the fire cannot be escaped! It will burn away all the "wood, hay and straw" of our lives as it purifies the "gold, silver and precious stones" of our soul. It will intimately unite us with Christ. It will either purify and unite us, or destroy us at the coming of Christ. The choice is ours: be united with Jesus, or run from him.

Do we see fire as a friend or an enemy? Does it unite or destroy? Do we trust that it will purify us through its heat? Do we see it as a way to become passionately united with our Crucified Lover? Or do we see it only as an enemy? If we see it as our friend, we will be able to embrace it so that its pain actually becomes our comfort, sweetness, and freedom from fear. If we run from it, we will remain in pain, bondage, and fear. ☐

Make Every Effort to Preserve Unity
Luke 12:54-59 (29:Friday)

When you are going with your opponent to appear before a magistrate, try to settle with him on the way. (v. 58)

Are we reconcilers or do we put up walls of division?

Paul says to the Ephesians, "Never let evil talk pass your lips; say only the good things men need to hear, things that will really help them." So often division comes from our lips. We speak negatively, or we gossip. We judge a person before we know all the facts. Then and there we inwardly cause a separation from that person. Once this is "conceived, it gives birth to sin, and when sin reaches maturity it begets death." Such talk can literally kill a relationship with a brother or a sister.

It also blocks the working of the Holy Spirit in our life. Paul goes on after speaking of such negativity to say, "Do nothing to sadden the Holy Spirit." Unity is a work of the Spirit. Paul says again to the Ephesians, "Make every effort to preserve the unity which had the Spirit as its origin and peace as its binding force."

In today's gospel Jesus rebukes his listeners for being able to read the signs of the earthly winds, but not being able to read the heavenly wind of the Spirit. "The wind blows where it will. . . . So it is with everyone begotten of the Spirit." We cannot really bring reconciliation without the work of the Spirit in our life.

But this does not mean we should be passive about making peace. Paul always mentions the work of the Spirit in connection with statements about active steps towards God. "Make every effort," he says in speaking of preserving the unity of the Spirit.

One of the best ways to actually stop speaking negatively about others is to actively start speaking only good things even about your enemies. If someone gets on your nerves, begin actively praising God for the good qualities they do have. Soon they will no longer really bother you, and you will be able to be a friend who lovingly supports them in working through any real faults.

"Enter his courts with songs of praise," says the psalmist. Such a habit of always praising God for a person's good points will stir up the real moving of the Spirit which will allow God to help them with their bad points. □

We Are All Sinners
Luke 13:1-9 (29:Saturday)

Do you think that these Galileans were the greatest sinners in Galilee just because they suffered this? (v. 2)

Do we think that those who suffer are being punished for their sins? Paul does say, "Whoever eats the bread and drinks the cup of the Lord unworthily sins against the body and blood of the Lord. A man should examine himself first. . . . That is why many among you are sick and infirm, and why so many are dying." Indeed, the Old Testament is full of examples of God punishing sinners with physical suffering and death.

Today, there is a new version of the gospel that says if you obey God you will never suffer, so those who suffer must not be obeying God. But what of Paul who says "I glory in my suffering"? To correlate all suffering with active sin in a person's life is just not consistent with the words of Jesus or the experience of the people who follow him.

Jesus does not ask whether they were sinners or not. He asks, "Do you think these Galileans were the greatest sinners in Galilee just because they suffered this?" Jesus is pointing out the total equality of our sin and our need for God. "All are now undeservedly justified by grace through the redemption wrought in Christ Jesus." He says of the vices which come from the evil spirits and the trends of the world, "All of us were once of their company." Do we try to justify our own sin by pointing out the greatness of the sin of others? It doesn't work. Adam tried it with Eve and Eve tried it with the serpent, yet all three were cast out from paradise.

Jesus does not leave it at this. "But I tell you, you will all come to the same end unless you reform your lives." Jesus calls us all to change. He is not some kind of "ear tickler" who comes to make us feel all warm and cozy, or to give us spiritual goose bumps. He challenges us with a gospel that calls us to radical change.

Sometimes this means changing the things we have grown quite accustomed to. He calls the rich young man to give everything to the poor. He tells us to cut off even our hands if they act not in accordance with the will of God. His words know no limit of familiarity or romantic attachment. He calls us to give up absolutely everything if we really want to follow him.

Do we judge others' sins when we ourselves refuse to change certain areas of our life? Do we realize the total equality of our poverty before God? Do we realize the totality of the response required by God? Jesus tells us if we sin in our thoughts and feelings we are already guilty of adultery. James tells us if we offend in one part of the law, we are guilty of offending against the whole law. We are all equal. One is not better than another. We are all sinners. We must all change. □

Facing Opposition Inside the Church
Luke 13:10-17 (30:Monday)

The chief of the synagogue [was] indignant that Jesus should have healed on the sabbath. . . . The Lord said in reply, "O you hypocrites!" (v. 14-15)

What do we do when we face opposition from the leaders of the church? So many times we are simply trying to heal someone, but because of church protocol we are hindered by the clergy. Worse yet, sometimes the clergy is so deeply mired in sin that they do not like it when a lay person comes along and rocks the boat with righteousness. This is the situation that faces many lay leaders and ministers in today's church.

Jesus says, "The scribes and Pharisees have succeeded Moses as teachers; therefore, do everything and observe everything they tell you. But do not follow their example." He then goes on to bring charge after charge upon them, calling them hypocrites in every case. Jesus says, "Do not think I have come to abolish the law and the prophets. I have come, not to abolish them, but to fulfill them." Yet he does break that law so that the Pharisees often rightly say of the disciples, "Look! Why do they do a thing not permitted on the sabbath?" Jesus honors the laws of the Jews of his day, but often overlooks their outer scruples in order to see and fulfill the deeper and more important meaning of the law. He honors the position of the teachers of the law, but often takes issue with the personal example of those who scrupulously keep the externals of the law while neglecting its very heart and spirit. He did not hesitate to get angry with them and even to call them hypocrites.

Even within the New Testament church Paul shows the same balance towards Peter. "When Cephas came to Antioch, I directly withstood him, because he was clearly in the wrong." Yet he also submitted his preaching to Peter, "I laid out for their scrutiny the gospel as I present it to the Gentiles—all this in private conference with the leaders, to make sure the course I was pursuing, or had pursued, was not useless. . . . Those who were acknowledged pillars, James, Cephas and John, gave Barnabas and me the hand clasp of fellowship."

Francis of Assisi likewise said, "We have been sent to help the clergy toward the salvation of souls. . . . Everyone will receive his reward, not according to the authority he exercises, but according to the labor he does. Know, brothers, the fruit of souls . . . can be better obtained by peace with the clerics than by disagreements with them. If they hinder the salvation of people, the revenge pertains to God and he will repay in due time. Therefore, be subject to prelates. . . . Hide their lapses, supply for their many defects, and when you have done this, be even more humble." Francis says in his Testament, "God inspired me, too, and still inspires me with such great faith in priests who live according to the laws of the holy church of Rome, because of their dignity, that if they persecuted me, I should still be ready to turn to them for aid. And if I were as wise as Solomon and met the poorest priests of the world, I would refuse to preach against their will in the parishes where they live. I am determined to reverence, love and honor priests and all others as my superiors. I refuse to consider their sins, because I can see the Son of God in them and they are better than I. I do this because in this world I cannot see the most high Son of God with my own eyes, except for his most holy Body and Blood which they receive and they alone administer to others."

How do we deal with the sin of the leaders of the church? Do we correct individual sin in a way that retains honor and reverence for their office? Do we really understand the deeply mystical dimension of honoring their office in the church? It is all right to get angry at this sin, but we must never be angry at the person who sins. It is also all right to point out the hypocrisy of a person, but we must never humiliate the office of leadership appointed by Christ. In doing this we humiliate Christ. Whatever we do, we must do it for the good of the people of God, the church. If we tear her down, we tear down the work of Christ. □

Be Faithful in Small Things
Luke 13:18-21 (30:Tuesday)

What does the reign of God resemble? (v. 18)

Do we find the great things of God in the little things of our life? It is sometimes easier to proclaim Jesus to the multitudes than to proclaim him to your own family. It is often easier to work for the poor in the inner city than to wash a dish or clean a room in your house in the suburbs.

Jesus says if we are faithful in the little things, we will be given the great things as well. We should sit in the lowest place, then we will be asked to come up higher.

The mustard seed "is the smallest of all, yet when full grown it is the largest of plants," says Jesus. "It becomes so big a shrub that the birds of the air come and build their nest in its branches," says Jesus, according to Matthew.

According to many commentators, this means that the kingdom will begin supporting the whole world! It will start out small and almost unnoticeable. It will grow and grow until it becomes the strongest and most stable structure in the whole world. Then those of the world will come to find support in "its branches."

The kingdom is like yeast, not dough. The yeast is small in comparison to the measure of flour to be used. Yet it is the yeast which keeps the whole dough from falling flat. It is the little yeast which enables the dough to become the bread which feeds the hungry.

If we are faithful in the little things, God will enable us to deal with the problems of all the world. Paul says a bishop should be a good family man before he is set over the family of the church. He says the same things regarding deacons. But if we are faithful in the little things of our own family life, then, and only then, can we lead others in keeping peace within the church and the world.

Are we loving and kind to those closest to us, or do we easily become irritated and short tempered with them? Are we Christ-like only with those we can keep at a distance: our prayer group, our parishioners, or the street people we serve? If we do all this without real love, it will come to nothing, but if we possess love even in the small things, our ministries can change the world. □

Jesus Challenges Us
Luke 13:22-30 (30:Wednesday)

Try to come in through the narrow door. Many, I tell you, will try to enter and be unable. (v. 24)

Jesus challenges us today. He stands like a football coach trying to get his team moving. Sometimes he encourages and supports, but at other times he must warn the team that they will lose the game if they do not do better in practice.

This life is much like a practice or a scrimmage before the real game. The real game comes after this life in the arena of eternity. If we do not really get to know the plays and the coach in the practice, we will be lost when we get to the real game. Jesus will say, "I tell you, I do not know where you come from. Away from me, you evildoers!"

It is not enough to dress up like a player and hang around on the field. We must take part in the warm-ups, learn the plays by heart, and come to know the mind of the coach. Jesus is our head coach, and the church is the team.

It is not enough to go through the motions of life for Christ. It is not enough to simply be present at prayers, we must really pray. It is not enough to casually receive the Bread of Life. We must ourselves be broken so that we might actually become bread for a hungry world. It is not enough to talk about Jesus, we must actually come to know Jesus. Then, and only then, do we really understand salvation.

Life in Christ is abundant, but life away from Christ is a living hell. Today Jesus warns us what life will be like without knowing him. "There will be wailing and grinding of teeth." Hell is a reality. Jesus warns us about its existence. He clearly tells us about our options for the future: life with him in abundance and joy, or life away from him in agony and pain. The choice is simple and clear. The choice is ours.

Yet he also tells us of the abundance of heaven: "People will come from the east and the west, from the north and the south.

... Some who are last will be first and some who are first will be last." Jesus' love knows no boundaries. He offers his love to us today. He warns us of life without him today. He challenges us to make a decision.   □

True and False Religion
Luke 13:31-35 (30:Thursday)

O Jerusalem, Jerusalem, you slay the prophets and stone those who are sent to you. (v. 34)

Jerusalem was, and is, a city centered on God. It is a city rampant with religion, yet it is a city which has traditionally rejected and killed the prophets God has sent to her.

Jesus was no exception. It was in Jerusalem that the crowds cried out to crucify him. It was in Jerusalem that Jesus found a hypocrite religion, weighed down by externalisms that suffocated the life of God in the simple and uneducated. Even in Jesus' day, Jerusalem was a city filled with religion, yet unable to really draw close to the living God.

Jesus spent most of his time in Galilee. Galilee is a region of lakes, open fields, and hills covered with flowers. It is a place where farmers, shepherds, and fishermen find God in the simple and beautiful things of life. Jesus spent most of his time there preaching, healing, and teaching the kingdom of God to the simple and the poor. Here he was accepted by a simple people in an honest lifestyle he embraced and loved.

Yet he set his face like flint towards Jerusalem. He ventured forth into the desert. He ventured forth into the city. He ventured forth to bring the freedom of the Spirit to a people in bondage to vain religion. Truly "no prophet can die outside of Jerusalem."

Is our life like Galilee or Jerusalem? "How often have I wanted to gather your children together as a mother bird collects her young under her wings." Do we accept this simple love of Jesus, or do we reject him through an endless maze of religious rules and rituals? Do we condemn Jesus because he breaks our religious laws, or do we accept his love which "covers a multitude of sins"?

Finally, do we venture forth from Galilee to Jerusalem? Are we really concerned about those dying of thirst in the desert, those unable to find holy silence and solitude in the city, and those entrapped in the prison of a religion which "has the form of godliness while denying its power"? We must be willing to be God's prophets, giving what we have received and willing to give our own life in the process, just as Jesus gave his life for us. □

God's Law and Human Tradition
Luke 14:1-6 (30:Friday)

Is it lawful to cure on the sabbath or not? . . . If one of you has a son or an ox and he falls into a pit, will he not immediately rescue him on the sabbath day? (v. 3, 5)

The Jews had a problem. Yahweh had given them the law, but the law was not specific enough. There were circumstances not mentioned in the law that were part of their daily experience. To meet this experience their spiritual leaders had developed the Mishnah. The Mishnah covered almost every conceivable circumstance in Jewish life and provided a specific, detailed answer. The law was from God. The Mishnah was from men. Yet the Mishnah was enforced with nearly the same emphasis as the law.

The Mishnah of the Jews is much like the canon law of the church. The gospel is our general law, and the canon law helps interpret the gospel in very specific situations in our modern world. Likewise, the Mishnah is to the Torah what constitutions and statutes are to a community rule. The problem is that often our community constitutions do not much resemble the original rule of the founder or foundress. We replace the simple clarity of a few brief pages with a massive book of rules, and then expect the people of God to be unburdened and free.

Many times these secondary documents are both too compromising and too burdensome. The original "law" cut like a surgical knife to bring healing. It spoke radical, almost unliveable gospel challenges, but anyone who chose to live these radical challenges found a freedom in the Spirit beyond description. This brought joy. The secondary documents, on the other hand, tend to be like an overweight athlete. The layer of fat might protect the athlete from external forces, but it slows them down in the race. The secondary documents tend to compromise the radical nature of the primary call in specific circumstances. At the same time, they can do away with any charismatic possibility of the Spirit leading in a particular situation. They often take joy and excitement from the spiritual life of a community.

The main thing to remember is that the secondary document comes from human sources, while the primary writing comes from God. God might inspire the secondary, but the primary is written by the very finger of his Spirit. It cannot change. The problem comes when we try to attribute the same level of inspiration on the second as on the first.

Jesus had clearly broken the tradition of the Mishnah. Jews could not do any work on the sabbath. Healing was considered work. Jesus had, therefore, transgressed. But Jesus would rather obey his Father in heaven than the ecclesiastical authorities on earth. Jesus was a good orthodox Jew and, no doubt, fulfilled the law and tradition in most things. In some matters, however, God's love had to prevail over human laws.

Jesus calls us back to the heart of the law. To "love the Lord your God" and to "love your neighbor as yourself" are the two commandments upon which the whole law is based. Paul says, "Love is the fulfillment of the law." Even in the rule that Francis of Assisi wrote in 1221 he admits of certain specifics, "Necessity knows no law." Of course, the quote from Augustine, "Love God and do what you will," remains true today as it did then.

Love itself tells you what to do in an emergency. Will you heal or inflict, save or destroy? You might have to break a community rule, or even a specific canon law to love, but true love will always be the better interpretation of the law, the gospel, or our rule of life.

Do we see our church canon laws and community constitutions as aides to following the gospel of Jesus Christ, or do we allow them to subtly replace the gospel? Are we filled with spiritual life and joy, or have we grown tired and laborious, like a dusty old lawyer? If we are not joyful, chances are we have confused our human writings for the gospel.

Canon laws and constitutions can be very helpful and good as long as they only serve as aids to living the gospel of Jesus. As soon as they become the gospel, they can bring spiritual death. Laws and constitutions have changed many times in the history of the church, but the gospel will remain forever. We should not build our life around something that will change and die. We should build our life on the word of God which stands forever. If we do this we will all be much happier. If we do this we will also live forever. □

Humble Yourself
Luke 14:7-11 (30:Saturday)

What you should do when you have been invited is go and sit in the lowest place, so that when your host approaches you he will say, "My friend, come up higher." This will win you the esteem of your fellow guests. (v. 10)

James says, "Be humbled in the sight of the Lord and he will raise you on high." He writes in the tradition of the Jewish wisdom literature which itself says, "My son, conduct your affairs with humility, and you will be loved more than a giver of gifts. Humble yourself the more, the greater you are and you will find favor with God."

How different this is from many western expressions of

Christianity. In the west we are told to be bold in order to minister to a culture indoctrinated with self-assertiveness. The preachers might say, "Love your neighbor as yourself," but they often emphasize "love yourself." Our preachers promise success and prosperity. They make much of our need for self-fulfillment and self-awareness. Seldom is self-sacrifice and self-emptying mentioned.

Paul says, "Your attitude must be that of Christ: Though he was in the form of God, he did not deem equality with God something to be grasped at. Rather, he emptied himself and took the form of a slave, being born in the likeness of man. He was known to be of human estate, and it was thus that he humbled himself, obediently accepting even death, death on a cross! Because of this, God highly exalted him."

Even with Jesus exaltation came only through humility. Even Jesus "learned obedience from what he suffered." There is no "end run" around the cross. If you are not willing to be humbled by the enemy's linemen, you can never reach the end zone to score a touchdown. By your own strength you cannot break through. It can only come through God's grace. Through the cross we know it is by grace. Through the cross and through grace we learn humility.

The Scriptures do say, "Let us confidently approach the throne of grace," and Jesus does say the gospel should be "proclaimed from the rooftops." We should not, however, forget that he also says to approach the throne of God with the humility of the tax collector, who "kept his distance, not even daring to raise his eyes to heaven. All he did was beat his breast and say, 'O God, be merciful to me, a sinner!' Or, as Peter says, "Should anyone ask you the reason for this hope of yours, be ever ready to reply, but speak gently and respectfully." Sirach even says, "Of forgiveness be not overconfident, adding sin upon sin. Say not, 'Great is his mercy; my many sins he will forgive.'". . . Delay not your conversion to the Lord.

Do we approach God in pride . . . even when we ask for forgiveness? Do we demand, or do we ask of God? Likewise, do we take our rightful place, or do we willingly take the least place with God and with others? Do we demand justice, or would we prefer to wait for mercy?

Often our justice will boomerang. Usually people do not think as highly of us as we think they should. Surely, if we approach God demanding justice we will end up condemning ourselves. Paul says, "No one will be justified in God's sight through observance of the law. . . . There is no just man, not even one." For the same reason he says, "Put away ambitious thoughts and associate with those who are lowly. Do not be wise in your own estimation."   □

The Glory of Heaven Awaits Us
Matthew 5:1-2 (All Saints)

When he saw the crowds he went up to the moutainside. After he had sat down his disciples gathered around him, and he began to teach them. (v. 1)

Jesus shows us that the key to blessedness in heaven is being faithful in the little things while still on earth. Nowhere on this list do we find a glorious scene of pomp and ceremony, no high liturgical splendor. Here we only find the mention of the meek and the lowly: the poor who cannot afford the fine vestments or ornate altars of the church. They seek God from the midst of such humble and mundane surroundings and because of this Jesus pronounces them among the saints and the blessed.

This is not to say that such glory and splendor should not be a part of our life. Jesus has promised us a heavenly dwelling where there are many mansions. The Book of Revelation tells us that we will worship God with all the saints in heavenly splendor and glory. We do have this hope of glory while still sojourning here on earth.

It is this hope which helps us live our life in holiness. As John's Gospel says, "Everyone who has this hope based on him

[Jesus] keeps himself pure, as he is pure." We know that in heaven we shall look upon God face to face and "we shall be like him, for we shall see him as he is." Awesome things await those who are faithful on earth. "Eye has not seen, ear has not heard, nor has it so much as dawned on many what God has prepared for those who love him." Yet God has revealed this wisdom to us through the Spirit.

If we are faithful to God in the humble things, then God's glory will actually be revealed through us. We have been given the Spirit. Even while we walk the face of the earth, we "are already seated in heavenly places in Christ." Our spirits already dwell in heaven in Christ, and we reveal glory through the spirit even while robed in flesh and the humble things of earth.

Are we aware of this awesome reality while carrying out the mundane activities of our day? Do we really seek out the activity of the Spirit throughout our day? As Francis says, "At all times and seasons, in every country and place, every day and all day" we must keep him in our hearts. And Clare says, "Place your soul before the mirror of eternity and glory of heaven even while on earth!"   □

Showing Hospitality to the Poor
Luke 14:12-14 (31:Monday)

Whenever you give a lunch or dinner, do not invite your friends or brothers or relatives or wealthy neighbors. They might invite you in return and thus repay you. (v. 12)

So many times in our churches and communities we become so preoccupied with the passage, "If man does not work, he should not eat," that we forget these words of Jesus. We will take vagrants and drifters, but only if they will work in exchange for our hospitality.

It often happens that our dinners and community gatherings are filled only with those we have invited. We invite only the people who seem safe, those who think like we think and act like we act.

The words of Jesus challenge these attitudes. Granted, it is good to give jobs to the poor, and it is good to have community gatherings and "agapes," but if this is all we do, we have fallen short of the gospel of Christ.

Jesus says we should invite the marginal members of society to our church receptions. And Paul says, "Look on the needs of the saints as your own; be generous in offering hospitality . . . associate with those who are lowly." We should rejoice that they cannot bring anything. They will not see things the way we do. They will not walk through life the way we do. They may not be as self-sufficient as we are. They may not fit into our Christian social life that so caters to the yuppie generation and middle class society.

But by inviting them into our presence we might discover that we are the ones who are truly blind. We are the lame and the crippled. God willing, we will discover that we, too, are beggars, not nearly as self-sufficient as we thought. We need God and we need others.

Are we willing to come out of our safe environment by allowing marginal people into our life? Do we really help people who cannot repay us? Do we really believe God will if we do? Are we willing to learn from the uneducated and the poor? Are we willing to find God even in a person who doesn't seem to know God? We should show hospitality to them for God has shown hospitality to us in Christ. □

All or Nothing
Luke 14:15-24 (31:Tuesday)

They began to excuse themselves one and all. (v. 18)

Do we constantly make excuses for not following Jesus without compromise? Do we say yes with our mouth and then no with our actions? I am afraid most of us follow this common pattern.

Notice that all the reasons for not following the call of Christ seem like good ones. Stewardship over land or concern for the family certainly seem like important matters. But Jesus tells us otherwise. He says, "If anyone comes to me without turning his back on his father and mother, his wife and his children, his brothers and sisters, indeed his very self, he cannot be my follower." Matthew includes "home, brothers or sisters, father or mother, wife or children or property." Jesus demands all or nothing. Nothing or nobody can stand between us and the call of Jesus.

Ironically, Jesus says the marginal people of the streets and alleys of the town will make better followers than the stable people who come with second thoughts. For street people, it is all or nothing. They live from day to day. The choices are always clear and the consequences are always immediate. Such people often understand the immediacy of Jesus' call much better than those who "trust in their possessions." Jesus says, "Go out quickly to the streets and alleys of the town and bring in the poor and the crippled, the blind and the lame."

Today we must realize that if we do not respond to God's call, God will call to someone else. "I want my house to be full," says the Lord. If we will not follow Jesus without compromise someone else will. If we are too proud, God will use the lowly. If we are too self-sufficient, God will use the poor. If we do not really think we need redemption, God will turn to the lame, the blind and the sick. They have no pretense about their need to be healed.

Are we ready to admit our need for God today? When he calls, will we understand the immediacy of our need, or will we be deceived by the seeming security of our environment? Today when Jesus calls us to follow, will we make feeble excuses or will we follow him without compromise? □

Are We Willing to Pay the Price?
Luke 14:25-33 (31:Wednesday)

If anyone comes to me without turning his back on his father and mother, his wife and his children, his brothers and sisters, indeed his very self, he cannot be my follower. (v. 26)

Today Jesus asks us to consider carefully what it takes to follow him. It is easy to get excited about Jesus when our emotions run high and those around us encourage a sugar-coated brand of Christianity. But today Jesus tells us what it will cost us to follow him. It will cost us our entire life!

We must renounce all of our possessions. We must be able to turn our back on all we hold dear: family, friends, even our very self. The self we are so comfortable with must be discarded so that Jesus can make us anew. The price of grace was Jesus' whole life. Now ours is required in return.

Jesus tells us in the parable of the sower that most of the seed scattered by the sower will not take root and grow. The rocky soil represents the people who will not allow the seed of God's words to penetrate deep into their life. The seed choked out by thorns represents the people who allow the cares and anxieties of this life to eventually take precedence over living according to Jesus' words.

So often we are like this. We will not really turn from the things of the world, so the world eventually chokes out the words of Jesus from our life. We like to talk about Jesus, but we do not let his words permeate our life. Jesus says this isn't enough.

Paul says, "You must put aside your former way of life and the old self which deteriorates through illusion and desire and acquire a fresh, spiritual way of thinking. You must put on the new man created in God's image." Or again, "Put aside your old self with its past deeds and put on the new man." He says of himself, "Those things I used to consider gain I have now reappraised as loss in the light of Christ. I have come to rate all as loss in the light of the surpassing knowledge of my Lord

Jesus Christ. For his sake I have forfeited everything. I have accounted all else rubbish so that Christ may be my wealth."

Are we willing to obey Jesus with Paul? Jesus has told us openly and clearly what it will really cost us to follow him. We have been given fair warning. Are we willing to respond? Or would we rather just be a social Christian who talks much but does little? A yuppie for Christ, who buys and sells all the latest items at the Christian bookstore, but will not give everything to the poor in obedience to his words? Are we serious, or are we playing a religious game? Jesus wants serious, committed followers who will lay down their whole lives in imitation of him. □

Evangelism Means Love
Luke 15:1-10 (31:Thursday)

I tell you, there will likewise be more joy in heaven over one repentant sinner than over ninety-nine righteous people who have no need to repent. (v. 7)

Jesus is not interested in numbers. He is interested in people. It is not enough to have zeal to evangelize the world. We must really care about people.

Today our world is filled with Christian evangelists, yet we still are not really reaching the world. We have tape ministries, book ministries, records, radio stations. Yet with all of our expensive and energy-consuming media we are not really reaching the world.

Francis of Assisi reached the world more dynamically than most of us involved in modern media. Mother Teresa of Calcutta seeks none of the media coverage, but she gets it without even trying. Why?

Both Francis and Mother Teresa care about people. They love. Famous people or God's "little ones," it makes no difference. They give the same time to both. If they heal in Jesus' name, they are first willing to heal in Jesus' way. They are willing to actually take the place of the poor and the sick in order to heal them. They really love the people they minister to, and love them deeply. Francis said that a real Christian leader must love his people so much that they would know they are forgiven and healed only by looking into the leader's eyes. I can tell you by experience that Mother Teresa possesses this quality herself.

The Pharisees had zeal to evangelize, but they did not do the will of God. Jesus said, "You frauds! You travel over sea and land to make a single convert, but once he is converted you make a devil of him twice as wicked as yourselves." It is not even enough to have zeal to win souls. Why? The scriptures say, "If I have not love, I am nothing."

Do we really love every person who comes into our life? Will we take time with the unimportant just as we would the important? Do we take time with them because we really love them as Jesus, even enough to take on their sufferings and problems? We must answer these questions before we can really evangelize in a way that will bring joy to the angels of heaven and can truly be called Christian. Is our media evangelism and door-to-door witnessing authentic, or is it just a holy fraud? Our evangelism media is good, but without the power of Jesus' love it is pointless and proud. Our door-to-door ministry is good, but without real care for the people who come to those doors it is a lot of work in vain. Will we evangelize like the Pharisee, or will we evangelize like Christ? □

Go, and Make Disciples
Luke 16:1-8 (31:Friday)

The worldly take more initiative than the other-worldly when it comes to dealing with their own kind. (v. 8)

How true this is! Be it mass media or one-on-one counseling, the secular world often does a better job than

Christians. There is certainly no question that the secular media reaches many more people with more creative campaigns than does the Christian media. Similarly, more people have certainly heard of Amway and have its products on their garage shelves than have really heard of Jesus from someone coming into their homes with a caring heart. There is no question. The secular world takes more initiative than does the Christian world.

But let us not forget, Jesus calls the steward in today's gospel reading a "wily manager," a "devious" entrepreneur. It is a backhanded compliment at best. Our initiative is not for self-gain; it is to be for love. "Love is the fulfillment of the law," says Paul in imitation of Jesus.

The scriptures are filled with injunctions to both live and spread the gospel with radical initiative. "Go out to the streets and the alleys" or "Go, therefore, and make disciples of all the nations," says Jesus. With the empowerment of the Holy Spirit the church began to spread like wildfire across the face of the earth. Jesus' words "I have come to set a fire on the earth" were quickly fulfilled by the initiative of the first Spirit-filled Christians.

We are to "be in the world but not of the world." That is why James says, "Looking after widows and orphans in their distress and keeping oneself unspotted by the world make for pure worship without stain before our God and Father."

Do we really take steps of initiative to radically follow Christ? Is our lifestyle changed by our desire to purely worship and look after those in poverty and distress? In our desire to take initiative for Christ have we sometimes compromised the purity of the gospel and become "devious" in our evangelism campaigns? Let us take initiative in stirring up the gift of the Holy Spirit in our life, then we will continue to fan into a full flame the fire Jesus ignited on the face of this earth! □

Little Things Lead to Great Things
Luke 16:9-15 (31:Saturday)

If you can trust a man in little things, you can also trust him in greater. (v. 10)

Here is the resounding theme of Jesus calling us to reverence the importance of the seemingly little things. For our world, big is better, but Jesus stands in stark contradiction to the standard of our world. "What man thinks important, God holds in contempt," says Jesus. The way of the world says big things are important, but Jesus says it is the little things that lead us to the great.

Notice Jesus does not say, "What man thinks important God does not think important." Jesus says God holds these things "in contempt." This is not some kind of passive response by God. God's response is active and heartfelt!

So much of our work for God is actually contemptible to God. We say we do it for God, but we really do it for personal gain and notice. "You cannot serve both God and money," says Jesus, yet we try to do it all the time. That is why our ministries often take on such different manifestations and complexions than the ministry of Jesus himself. It is important for us to know that while we do these things in Jesus' name, God actually holds them in active and passionate contempt!

Today I cannot help but realize that Jesus comes to us in a little morsel of bread and a tiny sip of wine. It is not even enough to feed a person for one day, yet God is pleased with this. "This is my beloved Son in whom I am well pleased, listen to him," says the Father.

This morsel of bread and wine is foolishness to the world ... not "big" enough to feed the poor, yet the poor attend mass every day and every week by the millions to be thus fed by Christ. The world holds this "waste" in contempt, yet God is pleased and the poor are fed. How ironic and just: the world holds the logic of faith in contempt, yet God holds the logic of the world in contempt. The two cannot be reconciled.

Do we try to compromise the purity of the gospel with the logic of the world? Do we say we minister for Jesus, but really minister for gain? Do we see the Lord God Almighty coming to us in even the smallest things? Today let us receive Jesus under the appearance of the morsel of bread and the sip of wine, then will we find him in every little aspect of life. Then will our ministry be conformed to his and the Father in heaven be greatly pleased. □

The Gift of Forgiveness
Luke 17:1-6 (32:Monday)

Scandals will inevitably arise. . . . Be on your guard. If your brother does wrong, correct him; if he repents forgive him. (v. 1, 3)

Today, Jesus connects the effectiveness of our faith with our ability to forgive our brothers and sisters.

"Scandals will inevitably arise," says the Lord. Our communities are made up of real people, so we will not always be perfect. We will sin. John's first letter says, "If we say, 'We have never sinned,' we make him a liar and his word finds no place in us." He goes on to say, "I am writing this to keep you from sin. But if anyone should sin, we have, in the presence of the Father, Jesus Christ, an intercessor who is just." So we will have to deal with sin in our communities. No matter how radical in ideals we might be, no matter how Spirit filled we seek to be, we will still have to deal with our own sinful humanity. Do not be surprised when this happens!

This does not mean we should continue in our sin. John also says, "If we say, 'We have fellowship with him,' while continuing to walk in the darkness, we are liars and do not act in the truth. . . . The man who claims, 'I have known him,' without keeping his commandments is a liar, in such a one there is no truth." As Paul says, "What then are we to say? 'Let us continue in sin that grace may abound?' Certainly not! . . . Do not, therefore, let sin rule your mortal body and obey its lusts." We must all make an honest effort to try and follow Christ. But when we stumble in this honest effort, we can be assured that Jesus will pick us up and set us on the path of righteousness again.

We must, likewise, lift up our brothers and sisters when they fall. Paul says, "If someone is detected in sin, you who live by the Spirit should gently set him right. . . . Help carry one another's burdens." He says again, "Bear with one another; forgive whatever grievances you have against one another. Forgive as the Lord has forgiven you." Francis of Assisi writes in his rule for his brothers: "They must take care not to become angry or disturbed because of the sin of another, since anger and disturbance hinder charity in themselves and others." He also says, "There should be no brother in the whole world who has fallen into sin, no matter how far he has fallen, who will ever fail to find forgiveness for the asking, if he will only look into your eyes." Nothing must hinder us in obeying today's words of Jesus, "If your brother does wrong correct him; if he repents forgive him." If your brothers and sisters turn back to you and say "I am sorry," forgive them.

This attitude frees the Spirit within us. It keeps us from being negative, critical and overly scrupulous with others. Such an attitude allows us to be joyful and thankful in all things. It brings peace. As Paul says, "Dedicate yourselves to thankfulness" or "The fruit of the Spirit is love, joy, peace." Such attitudes stir the Spirit and power in our life. It is this power which uproots the sin and negativity in our life.

Do we let the sin of others upset us and drag us down into negativity? Do we walk in a constant attitude of offering the positive gift of forgiveness? Is the mountain of our own sin being removed by our faith? If not, perhaps it is because we are not ready to offer to those around us what we, ourselves, wish to receive from God. □

We Are Useless Servants
Luke 17:7-10 (32:Tuesday)

When you have done all you have been commanded to do, say, "We are useless servants. We have done no more than our duty." (v. 10)

Most societies or cultures of Christendom have sifted the gospel through their own cultural understanding. This is sometimes bad, but it can be good in so far as it makes the gospel relevant for all cultures.

I am struck today that this gospel simply does not match up to our modern understanding of the good news. To call yourself a "useless servant" is not considered a mark of a good self-image by even Christian schools of psychology! If Jesus were to show up at our local parish and preach this sermon, or give a retreat with this theme, he would greatly provoke his listeners. Such a teaching would not be well received.

Even worse: Jesus uses an analogy that passively condones the use of servants by masters. He does not have the master offer equal hospitality to his servant, or, better yet, have the master serve his servant. Jesus might allude to such attitudes in other parts of the gospel, but here, when given a clear opportunity, he does not speak out against such inherently evil structures in the name of social justice. No doubt about it, the Jesus of the Gospels does not always fit the modern gospel of our church.

Paul, too, makes no attempt to right the obvious "errors" in the teachings of Jesus. He even says, "Let all parties think humbly of others as superior to themselves, each of you looking to others' interests rather than to his own." Speaking of servants and masters he says, "Slaves, obey your human masters with reverence, the awe, and the sincerity you owe to Christ." Regarding even the brutal and unjust government of Rome he writes, "You pay taxes for the same reason, magistrates being God's ministers who devote themselves to his service with unremitting care. Pay each one his due: taxes to whom taxes are due; respect and honor to everyone who deserves them." No doubt about it: Paul does not fit into the modern gospel of social justice either!

I do not write this to say that social justice and equal rights are wrong. I write this only to place our fight for Christian social justice squarely in the mystical tradition of the gospel of Jesus Christ. Jesus spoke of an inner glory that transcends all earthly limitations and shackles. Paul, too, spoke of a peace which passes all understanding and a mystical love which surpasses all knowledge. If we limit the gospel of Jesus Christ to the externals of pragmatic structures and law, then we have missed the whole point of the gospel!

Does the Jesus of the gospel really fit into our modern interpretation of the gospel? Would we accept Jesus if he spoke these words to us today, or would we reject him as they did even in the culture of his own day? Do we really understand the inner secret of the good news, or do we still seek a religion that is external?   □

In Everything Give Thanks
Luke 17:11-19 (32:Wednesday)

One of them, realizing that he had been cured, came back praising God in a loud voice. He threw himself on his face at the feet of Jesus and spoke his praises. This man was a Samaritan. (v. 15-16)

So it is so often in the church. We are all touched by Jesus. We are all cured. But it takes a foreigner, someone from outside the church, to really be thankful and praise Jesus in full voice.

Inside the church we are always "religious." We know that contemplatives are the spiritually mature, so we spend all of our time being reverent and quiet. Then some Christians come along with loud praise and charismatic exuberance, and we think them immature, mere beginners.

What has really happened is that we have taken Jesus for granted and grown spiritually proud before we have ever really known him. We say it is no big thing to be healed by Jesus. We can even rationalize it with modern psychological theory. Most important, we must not let anything disturb our religious veneer of contemplative peace and quiet. By all means, we must look mature to those around us.

Jesus stands in stark opposition to this common plague of quasi-religious pride. He is appalled that not one Jew comes back to him in the loud and exuberant thanksgiving and praise of the Samaritan. In turn the Samaritan is approved and justified by Jesus, while the others were not.

So in the church, often not one Catholic or Evangelical Christian will come back to Jesus with such thanks. Never would anyone raise their voice so loudly! Never would anyone use spontaneous gestures of praise that are not ritualized in the liturgy. Yet we must be willing to express such human spontaneity if we are to have a living relationship with Christ. Only then can we really be saved from the myriad of meaningless rubrics and rituals we call religion.

Thanksgiving and praise can break through all of the sin in our life and save us. Paul says, "Dedicate yourselves to thankfulness" and "in all things give thanks." The psalmist says, "Enter his gates with thanksgiving, his courts with praise." A sure way to break through the negativity and sin in our own life and stir up the gift of the Spirit is to intentionally thank God in all things, the good and the bad, for "all things work together for the good of those who believe."

It was this kind of faith that cut through the racial, cultural, and even religious barriers with the Samaritan and prompted Jesus to say, "Stand up and go your way; your faith has been your salvation."

We might be religious. We might even consider ourselves contemplatives and spiritually mature. But do we really know the guiltless response to Jesus that brings salvation? Do we have the attitude of positive thankfulness in all places and with all people, or do we experience the negativity of spiritual pride? Are we afraid to openly show our thanks to Jesus, or are we afraid of upsetting the local parish? We must learn from this foreigner who openly showed his thanks to Jesus with loud voice and unrestrained gestures, and thus came to know real salvation! □

Do It Today
Luke 17:20-25 (32:Thursday)

The reign of God is already in your midst. (v. 21)

We can spend so much time looking for the reign of God that we pass right by its presence in our daily life. We talk about what we will do for God after this or that obstacle or responsibility is taken out of the way. Or we fantasize about some romantic ideal of gospel living for the future, all the while missing the many opportunities for radical gospel living which cross our path today.

So often we externalize the conditions under which we can radically follow Christ. We look for this or that sign as conditions for becoming radical. We wait for the right leader to come along in the right place at the right time. Yet Jesus says, "You cannot tell by careful watching . . . neither is it a matter of reporting it is 'here' or 'there.'" The reign of God comes upon us in the little things of our daily life right now!

Getting radical for Christ is simply a matter of opening ourselves to the power of the Holy Spirit. The working of this is powerful in things both great and small. It knows no boundaries, no limitations. There is no sin too great to prevent its working. There is no task too small for its greatness, no relationship is beyond repair, no life beyond redemption. "The Son of Man in his day will be like lightning that flashes from one end of the sky to the other."

This "day" is yet in the future, but it is also today! "The reign of God is already in your midst," says the Lord! Speaking of today Jesus says, "Nothing is impossible with God." Speaking of today he says "The Father knows how to give the Holy

Spirit to those who ask." This gift, this power, is intended for you today!

Do we make excuses about getting serious about following Jesus? Do we really ask to be empowered by the Holy Spirit, today, or are we secretly afraid we will have to change our life too much? I challenge you to be courageous enough to step out and boldly follow Christ today. He will totally change your life, but he will change it for the better. Such openness to changes takes courage. Are you willing to take this risk?

"Encourage one another daily while it is still 'today' so that no one grows hardened by the deceit of sin." Let the Spirit free you from the deceit of sin with the power and awesome freedom of divine lightning. As the secular salesmen of the world say, "Do it today!" □

Don't Look Back
Luke 17: 26-37 (32:Friday)

As it was in the days of Noah, so will it be in the days of the Son of Man. . . . It was much the same in the days of Lot. (v. 26,28)

Don't look back! "Remember Lot's wife," Jesus says. If we flee from the things of this world and keep looking back it will destroy us. "You cannot serve both God and money," says the Lord, but so many of us still try.

We must make a clean break with the world, and then never go back again. This means changing the way we think about the so-called benefits and pleasures of this world. Paul says, "Those things I used to consider gain I have now reappraised as loss in the light of Christ. . . . I have accounted all else as rubbish so that Christ may be my wealth." Looking through the seeming beauty of materialism and sin he says, "You must lay aside your former way of life and the old self which deteriorates through illusion and desire and acquire a fresh spiritual way of thinking."

Today, Jesus mentions even the normal, daily realities of life this earth which can pull the loyalties of our heart from the things of heaven: "It was much the same in the days of Lot: they ate and drank, they bought and sold, they built and planted.... A man is on the rooftop and his belongings are in the house, he should not go down to get them.... Two women will be grinding grain together; one will be taken and the other left." Food and drink, property and business, or normal daily labor—none of it should prevent us from keeping our eyes fixed primarily on Jesus. Again Paul says, "Set your heart on what pertains to higher realms.... Be intent on things above rather than on things of earth."

If we set our eyes on heaven, then the relationships of the world will become means for joy rather than frustration. If we give up everything, then all creation will become ours. If we own nothing, then we will be everywhere at home! As Jesus says, "Everyone who has given up home, brothers or sisters, father or mother, wife or children or property for my sake will receive many times as much and inherit everlasting life."

Do we keep looking back to the things of this world as if they are of better quality than the things of heaven? Do not let these thoughts take root. Call them what they are: illusion. Just as the illusion of the devil's lie to Adam and Eve led to death, so will these concerns choke out the seed of the word of God within you and lead you to spiritual death. Beware! Be aggressive about stopping these thoughts before they take root in your heart. "If your right hand offends you, cut it off." The deeper the root, the more difficult to cut, but if you do not give these thoughts a chance to take root they can easily be removed. □

Pray Always
Luke 18:1-8 (32:Saturday)

He told them a parable on the necessity of praying always and not losing heart. (v. 1)

Do we pray always, or, do we lose heart? Oh sure, we pray. But do we pray always?

Paul echoes the intent of Jesus when he says, "Never cease praying," or, "Pray without ceasing," or, "Pray continually." To Timothy he says as well, "In every place the men shall offer prayers with blameless hands held aloft." To the Ephesians he says, "At every opportunity pray in the Spirit, using prayers and petitions of every sort." There is no doubt that Paul took the parable of Christ on praying always both seriously and literally.

But how can we pray always? How can we pray when we are surrounded by the anxieties and concerns of life? You cannot think about two things at once! Oh yes, we know Jesus says, "You cannot serve both God and money." But he also said we must remain "in the world," even saying, "If you cannot be trusted with elusive wealth, who will trust you with lasting?" Surely Jesus knows you can't pray and work in the world at the same time!

Perhaps the words of both Jesus and Paul can give us some practical insights. Notice that Paul doesn't just say, "Never cease praying." He says also, "Rejoice always, never cease praying, rendering constant thanks." Or to Timothy he says also, "Be free from anger and dissension." Or to the Ephesians not just "Pray constantly," but "Pray in the Spirit."

In order to live in a constant attitude of prayer, we must begin the constant practice of giving thanks. This constant attitude of thanks stirs up the Spirit and dispels all the darkness of anger and dissension. If we thank God for every situation and every person, good or bad, anxiety will disappear and our life will become a constant prayer. This is why Jesus says to pray always and not lose heart. In losing heart we become negative and depressed, which in turn becomes the breeding ground of anger, dissension and all works of the flesh which keep us from constant prayer. The scriptures say, "Enter his courts with thanksgiving and songs of praise." Today we should turn our negative thoughts around by a constant discipline of thanksgiving and praise. By praising and thanking God for every person and situation, we will suddenly discover that our whole day can be a prayer.   □

A Matter of Choice
Luke 18:35-43 (33:Monday)

What do you want me to do for you? (v. 41)

This is the question Jesus asks us today. We must search our hearts deeply for an answer. Sometimes our immediate answer is the best, rising up from the depths of our heart. Conversely, a carefully considered reply can be superficial.

What do we really want? We say we want to follow the way of Jesus, but we do not. We say we want to be radical for Christ, but we continue to compromise. We say we want holiness, but we continue to live lives that are unholy. We answer Jesus' question, but our lifestyle reveals that we do not really answer him with the truth.

As Jesus says, "You will know them by their deeds. . . . Any sound tree bears good fruit, while a decayed tree bears bad fruit. A sound tree cannot bear bad fruit any more than a decayed tree can bear good fruit. . . . You can tell a tree by its fruit." If we really want to bear good fruit, we will. However, the continued and habitual presence of bad fruit in the life of someone who claims they want to be good, betrays the hidden and dark reality that perhaps they really prefer the bad.

Psychologists say that most mental disorders are subconsciously chosen. The line between sanity and insanity is very fine, and most of us come very close to it from time to time. Those who cross over, often choose to let go of all ties with normalcy and stability. It is perhaps subconscious, but it is still a personal choice. Likewise, joy, happiness, and peace in life are really matters of choice. You can take two people with identical or similar sets of circumstances, and one will be happy while the other remains sad. Tragedy comes to all. Bad circumstances and events inflict us all. It is only those who choose to remain happy in the midst of it all who will eventually succeed. The fact is, some people actually want to be sick, so they choose to be!

But what of the apostle Paul who still found sin in his life? He says, "I do not do what I want to do but what I hate. . . . What happens is that I do not do the good I will to do, but the evil I do not intend." Sometimes the apparent choice or presence even of sin in our life indicates a deeper desire for the good. Sin is usually only an abuse of the good. It sometimes reveals the deeper desire for something good! Abuse of sexuality can indicate the need for an intimate companionship that can only be ultimately fulfilled in God. Abuse of food and drink indicates the need for gratification and pleasure which can only be filled by God. Sin, Paul says, is the misguided attempt to fill this empty space in our soul with the creation rather than with the Creator.

What is it we really seek today? If we want healing and salvation, Jesus will give it. But we must really want it! Down deep do we really want to change our life in order to follow Christ, or would we rather just remain as we always have been? Many say one thing with their lips, but when it comes to action they remain the same. Are we aware that most of life's blessings and curses are within the power of human choice? God will give us what we want! Finally, do we try to find the right answer by looking in the wrong place? Jesus is the answer. Only he can fill the emptiness and longing of our human soul.   □

Salvation Has Come to This House
Luke 19:1-10 (33:Tuesday)

I mean to stay at your house today. (v. 5)

Jesus visits us this very day. What will he find?

In Zacchaeus he found only a sinner. "He has gone to a sinner's house as a guest." Yet Zacchaeus was eager to have Jesus visit him. "He quickly descended, and welcomed him with delight." Are we really that eager to have Jesus visit us?

Zacchaeus was a tax collector and a wealthy man, yet he says, "I give half my belongings, Lord, to the poor. If I have defrauded anyone in the least, I pay him back four fold." He was a sinner in light of his trade, yet he lived more righteously than most of the so-called righteous of Israel. This prompts Jesus' comments, "Today salvation has come to this house, for this is what it means to be a son of Abraham."

What will Jesus find in our house? We claim to be his followers, but do we even live as righteously as Zacchaeus? Do we give even half of what Zacchaeus did to the poor? Are we honest in our business?

Zacchaeus was a tax collector. A sinner. He was an outcast from the children of Israel because he gave in to the unjust political regime of Rome. Yet Jesus does not condemn him. Jesus commends his honesty and charity, and then proclaims that this tax collector is a legitimate son of Abraham because he has understood the heart of the law despite his position as an outcast from the people of the law.

Why did Jesus come to Zacchaeus's house? It was because Zacchaeus first sought Jesus out. He ran ahead of the crowd. He climbed a tall sycamore tree. He made an extraordinary effort! Jesus noticed this effort, and responded to his desire.

Do we make similar efforts? Despite our "shortness," despite our sin, despite the scorn of those around us, do we make such efforts to see Jesus?

Zacchaeus the sinner puts the righteous of all ages to shame. He is more eager to see Jesus, and he has less to be afraid of when his life is seen by Jesus. A sinner, yet more righteous than the righteous. A traitor of the Jews, yet more truly a son of Abraham. A man whose simple faith transcended all the sins and barriers of the world. A man to whose household Jesus brings salvation.

Are we more like Zacchaeus or the people who judge him? "Everyone began to murmur." Do we murmur against the righteous who do not fit our cultural expectations of religion or do we practice a charity and guileless honesty which transcends all cultures, all peoples, all jobs and all political positions? Jesus calls us to see beyond into this transcendent world of Spirit and truth. □

Be a Total Disciple
Luke 19:11-28 (33:Wednesday)

Whoever has will be given more, but the one who has not will lose the little he has. (v. 26)

How strange is this Jesus! Sometimes he calls us to give up all the things of the world. At other times he tells us if we don't use these things well, even cunningly, we will not be given the things of the kingdom. He is a paradox, beyond all our attempts to classify and categorize him.

Jesus says, "The wind blows where it will. You hear the sounds it makes but you do not know where it comes from, or where it goes. So it is with everyone begotten of the Spirit." Paul says, "The spiritual man appraises everything, though he himself can be appraised by no one."

Jesus does say, "You cannot give yourself to God and money," and calls his apostles to "sell everything and give to the poor." He also says, "If you cannot be trusted with elusive wealth, who will trust you with lasting wealth?" He even praises the initiative and the cunning of the devious of the world.

Jesus invites "the beggars and the crippled, the lame and the blind" to the wedding banquet. He invites into the kingdom the "bad as well as good." But those who do not reverence the invitation by being properly dressed are "bound hand and foot and thrown out into the night."

Jesus expects us to respond properly to his call. He expects us to do something with his gift to us of a new beginning. He expects us to change and reform our life, and become a total disciple! Paul says, "Make no mistake about it: no fornicator, no unclean or lustful person—in effect an idolator—has any inheritance in the kingdom of Christ. . . . You must lay aside your former way of life and acquire a fresh, spiritual way of thinking. You must put on the new man created in God's image." Jesus himself begins his ministry proclaiming, "Reform your lives! The kingdom of heaven is at hand!"

If we reform in basic things, God will give us greater things. If the seed of God's word takes root in our life without being choked out by the thorns of this world or sprouting in rocky soil which has no spiritual depth, then it will yield "a hundred or sixty or thirty fold." Jesus says, "If you had faith the size of a mustard seed, you could say to this sycamore 'Be uprooted and transplanted into the sea' and it would obey you." Or again, "The man who has faith in me will do the works I do, and far greater than these."

Do we do the works of Jesus himself? Do we do even greater works than his? If we do not, then perhaps we are not being faithful in the small things. Get radical in cutting out these obvious sins from your life, then God will do far greater things through you than you could ever dream or imagine. The time to start is now!   □

The Peace That Jesus Brings
Luke 19:41-44 (33:Thursday)

If only you had known the path to peace this day; but you have completely lost it from view! (v. 42)

How amazing! Jerusalem, the city of peace. Jerusalem, the city of the temple of God. Yet the Jews had turned their "house of prayer into a den of thieves," and were unable to find the path of peace. They were totally entrenched in religion that sought to infiltrate politics. Religious sects and reforms all had their part to play in the political and military structure of the land, yet the people were unable to find peace.

The zealots were in favor of establishing social justice by use of force if need be. They believed the Messiah would set up a kingdom of peace by force. The Pharisees and the Sadducees took a more moderate view by working within the controlling political systems to achieve their final goal of independence. Both believed in a peace that could be established by political persuasion and even military control and force.

Jesus stands in stark opposition to both. He disappointed both. The Jews wanted peace and justice. They wanted it to last, and they wanted it immediately. Jesus teaches us to love our enemies and not to resist our oppressors with physical force. He teaches of a kingdom that is not of this world, which effects the material world only with the force of prayer. The Jesus of the gospel greatly disappointed the political and social activists of his day. He was a failure in their eyes.

Why do the activists of our day continue to appeal to Jesus to justify their disobedience and their violence? Violence only breeds violence. The sword cannot stop the use of the sword. Can they not hear the words of Jesus which say, "Give to Caesar what is Caesar's and give to God what is God's." That is why Paul says, "Let everyone obey the authorities that are over him ... the man who opposes authority rebels against the ordinance of God. . . . You pay taxes for the same reason." He says this to a people oppressed by the unjust government of Rome!

The peace which Jesus brings "surpasses all understanding." It transcends and permeates all the people and nations, all political systems and governments, the unjust as well as the just. It brings riches to the wealthy and to the poor and showers down the Bread of Heaven on both the hungry and the full. It is internal and dependent on nothing external, yet it transubstantiates all creation in Christ.

No doubt, we must "make justice our aim; redress the wronged, hear the orphan's plea, defend the widow." We must remember that "it is better to obey God than man." Yet we must never forget that Jesus said, "If my kingdom were of this world my subjects would be fighting to save me from being handed over to the Jews. As it is, my kingdom is not here."

This is the path of peace spoken of by Jesus, a path of love, forgiveness and non-resistance. It is because the Jews did not understand this path that "they will wipe you out, and leave not a stone on a stone because you failed to recognize the time of your visitation." Will the religious peace movement of today meet with the same fate? □

Commercializing God's House
Luke 19:45-48 (33:Friday)

My house is meant for a house of prayer, but you have made it a den of thieves. (v. 46)

Perhaps this is why the Jews could not perceive the path of peace spoken of in yesterday's gospel. They had externalized and commercialized even their place of prayer, so they had come to externalize and politicize God's peace. They had missed the internal, so God would never give them the external.

Ironically, God will give external graces if we first seek the internal ones. "Seek first his kingship over you, his way of holiness, and all these things will be given you besides." But we must also have a real detachment from the external before we can find the internal. "You cannot give yourself to God and to money. What man thinks is important, God holds in contempt." Or, "If anyone comes to me without turning his back on his father and mother, his wife and his children, his brothers and sisters, indeed his very self, he cannot be my follower." Yet he goes on to say there is no one who has given these things up in detachment "who will not receive in this present age a hundred times as much—and persecution besides—and in the age to come, everlasting life."

Without internal prayer we can never have lasting peace. We cannot have real prayer with such a gross commercialization of spirituality.

And what about today? Never before has there been such an overflowing torrent of Jesus "junk." Today we must return to a reverential use of our houses of prayer. It is fine to have books available as a ministry and service to the people of God, but commercialization in God's name will surely bring down God's wrath!

Is our present abundance God's gracing of externals because we have sought only the internal? Are we truly detached and poor in spirit? Or have we simply set up an abundance of money changers' tables in the house of the Lord? We cannot have peace until we pray, and we cannot pray without overturning these money changers' tables within our own hearts and souls, as well as within our local house of prayer. □

Jesus Was Celibate
Luke 20:27-40 (33:Saturday)

The children of this age marry and are given in marriage, but those judged worthy of a place in the age to come and of resurrection from the dead do not. . . . They are sons of God. . . . God is not the God of the dead but of the living. All are alive from him. (v. 34-36, 38)

So often the people of today's church treat those who choose not to marry as if there were something wrong with them. They treat them as if they were not fully human until they are married. They treat them as if they were dead!

The Jews of Jesus' day had a similar belief. The Jews believed a man was not complete until he was married. This is based on the scriptures that say, "God created man in his image; in the divine image he created him; male and female he created them. God blessed them saying, 'Be fertile and multiply.'" Marriage was a way both to further complete the divine image through union of male and female, and a way to be fruitful and multiply. Until a man married, he was not considered really whole.

Jesus stands in sharp contrast to both the belief of the Jews and this subtle return to Judaism within contemporary forms of Christianity. In Matthew's Gospel Jesus says, "You are badly misled because you fail to understand the Scriptures and the power of God." He rebukes the Sadducees not only for failing to believe in resurrection, but for placing the standards of the present age over the eternal principles of heaven. It was wrong to place the temporary standards of animal reproduction and death over the principles of eternal life. Heaven cannot be clearly perceived until we let go of the standards of this age! Once we do this, then all the created world again reflects the realities of heaven!

Jesus himself was a celibate. He came into this world as a man to fully reflect the heavenly way of heaven. Jesus says, "Some there are who have freely renounced sex for the sake of God's reign. Let him accept this teaching who can." John the

Baptist, too, was celibate. The early church believed Mary to have remained a virgin all her days. Paul goes into the practical considerations of both marriage and celibacy: "The unmarried man is busy with the Lord's affairs, concerned with pleasing the Lord; but the married man is busy with this world's demands and occupied with pleasing his wife. . . . To sum up: the man who marries his virgin acts fittingly; the one who does not will do better."

The New Testament example, therefore, breaks radically with the understanding of the Jews concerning celibacy. Instead of being looked down upon as incomplete or inferior, celibacy is actually exalted. It frees people from the rightful concerns of raising a family to devote all their time to the family of God. It stands as a constant prophetic reminder of the temporary state of this world and, as such, it reminds us of our eternal state in heaven. It is a sacrifice, but it is a sacrifice made sweet through hope. It is sometimes lonely. But even in the loneliness we have the consolation of knowing we share intimately with Jesus by literally imitating his life on earth. Thus do we hope to share with him in heaven.

Do you really have a Christian outlook on celibacy, or have you reverted to a theology of the Jews? Do you consider celibacy a viable option, or has the sexual promiscuousness of this age made sexual activity a must for your life? Have you considered the celibate option as a vocation? If you have not considered it, you should, either for yourself or for others. It is the literal way of Christ.   □

She Gave Everything
Luke 21:1-4 (34:Monday)

They make contributions out of their surplus, but she from her want has given what she could not afford—every penny she had to live on. (v. 4)

Do we give from our surplus or from our want? Giving from our surplus is certainly commendable, but it is not as commendable as giving from our want. Jesus saw the rich and he saw the poor widow putting their offerings into the treasury. Undoubtedly the rich put in large amounts while the widow put in only two copper coins. Yet Jesus says, "I assure you, this poor widow has put in more than all the rest."

Paul speaks about both the "good" and the "better" ways. "The relief of others ought not to impoverish you; there should be a certain equality. Your plenty at the present time should supply their need so that their surplus may one day supply your need, with equality as the result." This is a very good and practical way within the basic Christian community. This was the way of the first Christian community of Acts where "everything was held in common . . . nor was there anyone needy among them, for all who owned property or houses sold them and donated the proceeds."

Paul also speaks of the better way: "In the midst of severe trial their overflowing joy and deep poverty have produced an abundant generosity. According to their means—indeed I can testify even beyond their means—and voluntarily, they begged us insistently for the favor of sharing in this service to members of the church." Paul supports this kind of generosity by the example of Jesus himself. "How for your sake he made himself poor though he was rich, so that you might become rich by his poverty."

The problem is that we rarely follow even the good way, much less the better! No doubt, Jesus calls us to the higher way. No doubt, Paul calls us to the high, if not the highest way. Yet we rarely respond to either call.

Do we even begin to "hold all things in common" with our brothers and sisters so that all might be financially sound? Usually we do not. Do we even rarely give out of our want, becoming poor ourselves so that others might be rich? Most likely we have never really done so.

Today Jesus calls us to the higher way. We must give as we have received. We must follow his example. We must give, not only from our surplus, but from our want and means. Only then can we claim to really imitate Jesus who "made himself poor though he was rich, so that others might become rich by his poverty." Only then can we learn the riches of selfless love. □

Fewer Churches, More Christians
Luke 21:5-11 (34:Tuesday)

Some were speaking of how the temple was adorned with precious stones and votive offerings. He said, 'These things you are contemplating—the day will come when not one stone will be left on another, but it will all be torn down.' (v. 5-6)

How quickly we forget these words of Jesus! We build churches and shrines, one after the other, until the countryside is dotted with them. Yet true Christlike attitudes and spirituality remain hard to find. Would that we had fewer churches and more Christians!

This is an old problem. The Lord said to David, "Should you build me a house to dwell in? I have not dwelt in a house from the day on which I led the Israelites out of Egypt to the present, but I have been going about in a tent undercloth. In all my wanderings everywhere among the Israelites, did I ever utter a word to anyone of the judges whom I charged to tend my people Israel, to ask: Why have you not built me a house of cedar?" On the Mount of Transfiguration Peter wanted to build three booths, but was cut off by the overwhelmingly mystical presence of the bright cloud. As Stephen said in his great discourse, "Yet the Most High does not dwell in buildings made by human hands."

It is not bad to have a church building, but it is bad to tie your whole understanding of God to a church building. Jesus said to the Samaritan woman who tried to limit the worship of God to a place, "Believe me, woman, an hour is coming when you will worship the Father neither on this mountain nor in Jerusalem . . . God is Spirit, and those who worship him must worship him in Spirit and truth." Paul said to the Galatians, "How can you return to those powerless, worthless, natural elements to which you seem willing to enslave yourselves once more? You even go so far as to keep the ceremonial observance of days and months, seasons and years! I fear for you; all my efforts with you may have been wasted."

It is not bad to worship Jesus in a church, but it is bad to think you can only properly worship Jesus in a church. Likewise, it is not bad to receive communion daily, but it is bad to think you will only really know Jesus if you receive communion daily. Such a belief indicates that we do not know him or worship him at all!

Do we overly emphasize the importance of ritual in our relationship with Jesus? Ritual is good if it leads us to the freedom of Jesus. It is bad if it limits the freedom of Jesus. Very often the strong inclusion of ritual leads to an over dependence on ritual, rather than a true dependence on God. We end up bound by ritual and judging others by our scrupulosity. We end up imprisoning others and remain imprisoned ourselves. Let us worship God in Spirit and in truth. Then the truth will set us all free! Let us remember that eventually the elements will melt with a fervent heat, and "not one stone" of our churches and shrines will be left on top of another. □

We Need Patience
Luke 21:12-19 (34:Wednesday)

By patient endurance you will save your lives. (v. 19)

Are we really patient? When all the world crumbles around us are we still secure in our life with God? James says, "Count it pure joy when you are involved in every sort of trial. Realize that when your faith is tested this makes for endurance. Let endurance come to its perfection so that you may be fully mature and lacking in nothing." Do we meet adversity with this joy which brings patience in the maturing process we all go through?

It is like laying stones: At first you build with joy and rigor in newness and excitement of building something of quality and worth. Later, however, you are tired, hungry and just ready to quit. But you keep going until the end by the faith and hope that you will soon complete the good work you began. You believe it will be well worth the effort.

The same holds true for building with spiritual stones in the temple of our life in the Spirit. At first our zeal and love makes following Jesus easy. But after a few years we grow weary and the thrill of following Jesus leaves us. It is at this time that our faith is really tested. We are tired. We are hungry. We are ready to quit and go home. But by faith we know even though it might not "feel good" to follow Jesus, that we must go on and let God complete his work in our life. We must continue by faith rather than feelings so that our faith might be made strong. Then our faith will support us regardless of our feelings.

In today's gospel Jesus promises us that we will be tested. "They will manhandle and persecute you, summoning you to synagogues and prisons, bringing you to trial before kings and governors, all because of my name." This very day our brothers and sisters in not-so-distant lands are being persecuted for their faith in Jesus and for their lifestyle which challenges the inherent injustice and evil of particular governments. Sadly enough, sometimes this persecution comes from religious leaders who slander God's little ones in the name of God and who accuse Jesus' disciples even in the name of Christ! But the Spirit strengthens our brothers and sisters, who are able to give witness even in the midst of such trial.

Are we willing to give witness on account of Jesus? We "have not yet resisted to the point of shedding blood." Are we willing to shed our blood for Jesus who first shed his blood for us? Do we find a calm and patient endurance in the midst of physical persecution which brings peace to our soul and gives witness to the work of the Spirit within? If not, then we are missing a key essential to following Jesus. We do not love him as he first loved us. We are not patient. We will never mature.   □

Stand Fast and Give Thanks
Luke 21:20-28 (34:Thursday)

When these things begin to happen, stand erect and hold your heads high, for your deliverance is near at hand. (v. 28)

How different this reaction is from the prediction that "men will die of fright in anticipation of what is coming upon the earth." The same set of troubles befall both groups of people, yet some will respond in hope while others die of fright.

Paul speaks of the day of the Lord "coming like a thief in the night," and says, "Therefore comfort and upbuild one another." Predictions of these catastrophic disasters are not meant to frighten us; they are meant to bring us comfort by assuring us that God still has everything under control. Paul says, "You are not in the dark, brothers, that the day should catch you off guard." We have been warned out of love so that we might be ready.

The world around us can seem a pretty dismal place. Every generation of Christians has thought things so bad that the last days were at hand. Sometimes it seems too much to bear! Yet Paul says, "No test has been sent you that does not come to all men." God will not let you be tested beyond your strength. Sometimes it seems that our trials and sufferings must be worse than anyone else's. Peter says, "Realize that the brotherhood of believers is undergoing the same sufferings throughout the world." The troubles and trials are universally the same. Only the way we deal with them makes them seem better or worse.

I don't mean to imply that everything will always be rosy. When Lazarus died, Jesus wept. Paul says, "We are afflicted in every way possible ... full of doubts, but we are not crushed ... we never despair." Even in the midst of his anxiety Paul goes on to thank God. He finds relief by living according to his own words: "Dedicate yourselves to thankfulness."

This is really the difference! One man grumbles and another chooses to give thanks. Both experience the same trouble, yet one is redeemed and another is lost. Peter and Judas both denied Christ: one's sorrow led to repentance and salvation, while the other's led to despair and damnation. Two men in the same trouble—one looks to Jesus in hope while the other turns from Jesus in despair.

Which will we choose today? As Jesus says, "Stop worrying about tomorrow. Today has troubles enough of its own." Will we meet those troubles with hope and thanksgiving or with despair? Your response will make all the difference as to whether Jesus will find you ready when he returns. As Peter says, "Do not be surprised that a trial by fire is occurring in your midst. It is a test for you, but it should not catch you off your guard. Rejoice instead, in the measure that you share Christ's sufferings. When his glory is revealed, you will rejoice exultantly." □

God's Word Is Alive
Luke 21:29-33 (34:Friday)

The heavens and the earth will pass away, but my words will not pass. (v. 33)

How permanent are the promises of God! How penetrating is his word! "God's word is living and effective, sharper than any two-edged sword. It penetrates and divides soul and spirit, joints and marrow; it judges the reflections and thoughts of the heart." "Your word is a lamp for my steps, O Lord."

Do we really meditate on the words of Jesus? The scriptures say, "Meditate on the law of the Lord day and night." Jesus explains the scriptures to us so we might find him within them. "Beginning, then, with Moses and all the prophets, he interpreted for them every passage of Scripture which referred to him." With the two disciples he taught, we can say, "Were not our hearts burning inside us as he talked to us on the road and explained the Scriptures to us?"

Does our heart burn when we hear the word of God, or does scripture seem boring and dull? Is the word of God living and effective for us?

If not, we are probably trying to read without the action of the Holy Spirit. Bonaventure says, "Let us not believe that it is enough to read without unction. . . . Enlightened though a man may be by natural and acquired knowledge, he cannot enter into himself, there to 'take delight in the Lord,' except through Christ. . . . Such a motion is something mystical and no one desires it unless the fire of the Holy Spirit inflames him to the very marrow."

The word of God will not cut "between soul and spirit, joint and marrow," unless the Spirit "inflames us to the very marrow." The Spirit guides us into all truth and reminds us of all the words of Jesus. It is the same Spirit which impelled and influenced the prophets.

As I have said so many times before, the Spirit must be "fanned into a full flame." We must "stir into flame" the gift of the Spirit in our life. This fire of the Spirit came as tongues of fire upon the first apostles and disciples gathered in the upper room.

We must not separate the study of God's word from the fire of God's Spirit in our lives. Do you pray in tongues or enter God's court with praise and thanksgiving before you meditate on God's word? If you do not, you should. It is the best way to stir up the Spirit to teach you inwardly while you meditate on the word of God with your mind. Tongues will cease and songs of thanksgiving will fade away, but the Spirit who brings us the word will endure forever. Without the Spirit we cannot know this word as a living word.

Otherwise our study and use of God's word will be dead and burdensome, line upon line and precept upon precept, so that we cannot even walk under the weight of it. But with the Spirit, God's word will be a lamp for our steps and a clear truth that will set us free!

Scriptures say only faith, hope and love will last forever. Everything else will pass away except Jesus' words. Let our Spirit-led study take us past all else, so we may grab hold of the faith, hope and love which last forever. □

Resist the World
Luke 21:34-36 (34:Saturday)

Be on guard lest your spirits become bloated with indulgence and drunkenness and worldly cares. (v. 34)

Do we let the cares and anxieties of life choke out the seed of the living word in our daily life? Do we let little worldly things creep into our life one by one until we find our whole life filled with worldliness?

It starts in little things, a slip of the tongue here, or too much to eat or drink there. Soon we find our whole life an array of undisciplined and selfish indulgence of the flesh. What began as a resolute answer to Jesus' call on our life is suddenly falling headlong back into a worldly and secular life!

"Pray constantly to stand secure before the Son of Man," says Jesus. The way to overcome this worldliness is by winning the battle of the mind, and the only way to win the battle of the mind is through constant meditation and prayer. Unless we live a life of prayer, we cannot overcome a life of worldliness and self-indulgence.

"Whatever a man thinketh, so he is," says Proverbs. "Meditate on the law of the Lord day and night," says the Psalms. Paul says, "You must lay aside your former way of life and old self which deteriorates through illusion and desire and acquire a fresh spiritual way of thinking." The illusion of sin takes place in the mind, and the reality of the spiritual life takes place in the mind. The battle front of our lifestyle unquestionably takes place in both the controlled and wandering thoughts of the mind.

James says, "The tug and lure of passion tempts every man. Once passion has conceived, it gives birth to sin, and when sin reaches maturity it begets death." Passion enters our soul through our thoughts. Once we embrace these thoughts and make them our own, they conceive in our soul and give birth to action in our daily life. It might take days, weeks, months, or years, but eventually such thoughts will change us into conformity with the illusions and passion and indulgence. If these run rampant in our life, death will begin to take shape in our very flesh. We will grow gluttonous, fat, addicted, unhealthy, sick and perhaps even terminally ill and diseased. Do not be deceived: sin brings forth death! Death to the spirit. Death to the emotions of the soul, and even death to the flesh.

"Finally, my brothers, your thoughts should be wholly directed to all that is honest, pure, admirable, decent, virtuous, or worthy of praise," says Paul. The only way to do this is by "praying constantly," says Jesus in today's gospel. "Pray in the Spirit at all times," says Paul, or, "Dedicate yourselves to thankfulness." If we do this, we will "enter the courts of the King" even while we walk the face of this earth. If we do this, the Day of the Lord that Jesus speaks of in this gospel will not "close in on us like a trap," rather, it will be our "day of deliverance." It will, nonetheless, "come upon all who dwell upon the face of the earth." As to whether it will be a trap or a day of deliverance depends on how we live our life. How we live our life depends on how we think and pray. The choice is ours. □

Expectant Faith
Matthew 8:5-11 (Monday, First Week Advent)

Many will come from the east and the west and will find a place at the banquet in the kingdom of God. (v. 11)

Jesus is truly a light to the Gentiles! He comes to dispel the darkness of the whole world and to fill it with his marvelous light. This is a time of expectation. This is a time of hope! A time of joy is coming to us!

The Jewish people of Jesus' day had grown accustomed to religion. A constant flow of self-proclaimed prophets, messiahs, and rabbis traveled the countryside preaching in their synagogues and in the temple. Healers were common. Many baptized their disciples as a sign of adult conversion. Yet it had all grown rather commonplace.

The centurion was not a Jew. He was a Gentile in a new land. He was probably not used to the healers and preachers he saw in this strange land. He had heard of Jesus and knew that he taught a new doctrine of love and healed the sick.

When his servant grew deathly ill, the centurion went to Jesus. He did not take Jesus for granted. All he knew was that Jesus had healed. Therefore he could surely heal his servant. He heard, he saw, and he simply believed.

For the centurion, faith was still something fresh and new. He was both more expectant and more reverent of Jesus than many of the Jews who followed Jesus' ministry with interest. He did not demand that Jesus come to his house, nor did he even think it necessary for him to come to his servant in order to heal him. For the centurion Jesus' word was enough!

Do we take Jesus for granted? Do we make arrogant demands on Jesus and approach him irreverently? If we develop a real sense of reverence, we will come with a humble sense of expectation and never take his healing for granted. It will be always new and wonderful for us!

Will we approach Christ today like a Gentile or like a Jew? Will it be enough for us simply to hear the word of God to believe, or will we doubt and demand some extraordinary visit from Jesus? If we come like this Gentile to "climb the mountain of God . . . to Zion from which will go forth the word of instruction," then as with the centurion, Jesus will show much amazement and will remark, "I assure you, I have never found this much faith in Israel." ☐

The Simple Live Radically
Luke 10:21-24 (Tuesday, First Week Advent)

What you have hidden from the learned and the clever you have revealed to the merest children. (v. 21)

Jesus is the long expected Savior. The prophets foretold his coming, and kings foreshadowed his reign. Wise men searched the scriptures to learn all they possibly could so that they would know him when he appeared. Jesus came to fulfill all the prophecies and wisdom of old.

Yet it was not the learned and the clever who recognized him at first. It was workers, and fishermen, the childlike and simple. "You have revealed to the merest children," exclaimed Jesus in an outburst of charismatic praise.

Paul says of the first church at Corinth, "Consider your situation. Not many of you are wise; not many are influential; and surely not many are well born. God chose those whom the world considers absurd to shame the wise; he singled out the weak of this world to shame the strong. He chose the world's lowborn and despised, those who count for nothing, to reduce to nothing those who were something; so that mankind can do no boasting before God."

Today is no exception. Our religious orders and seminaries are filled with the wise, but it is often the "on fire" simpletons who bring the gospel to the poor and who really find Jesus in the world.

This has often been the case throughout history. The educated speculate about the accomplishments of the simple and think they gain merit in this. We sit in our classrooms and boast about the radical accomplishments of the saints of the past, and then send our ministers so weighed down by so-called rules of moderation that they never rise above a dull mediocrity. They might want to, but in the end they simply cannot. All the while it is the simple and unlearned who are free to live radically for Christ.

We do not even allow the simple into our seminaries and religious orders, yet it is often they who live the gospel more radically and evangelize more effectively. We screen out the extremists, so that all we are left with are those willing to follow along with the program. Therefore, our church comes more to resemble the dull and mundane structures and activities of a secular corporation than a radically enlivened kingdom of God empowered by the fire and zeal of the Holy Spirit!

Have we become the learned and the clever, or are we still opening ourselves to the radical call of Jesus Christ like mere children? Do we speculate and study about Jesus so much that we never really end up following Jesus? Let us return to the innocence of childhood and remain radical for Christ! □

God Will Feed Us
Matthew 15:29-37 (Wednesday, First Week Advent)

Large crowds of people came to him bringing with them cripples, the deformed, the blind, the mute, and many others besides. (v. 30)

What a strange entourage! Jesus was travelling from village to village, collecting more disciples at each stop. It began with the twelve, then it was the seventy-two and the women who accompanied them. Next came a veritable multitude. Thousands of people dropped everything to follow Jesus. They had heard his call to abandon everything, so they did. Can you imagine the excitement and expectation of these people who left their jobs and families to wander around in poverty with this itinerant Messiah?

The crowd became hungry. Jesus had gone up onto the moutainside as was his custom, and the crowd had followed him. What could be done with this refugee camp of crippled and hungry people? Had they taken Jesus too literally in following him? Something had to be done!

God provided for those who responded with such radical and complete faith. First for the sick: "They laid them at his feet and he cured them." Next for the hungry: Jesus said, "My heart is moved with pity for the crowd. By now they have been with me three days, and have nothing to eat. I do not wish to send them away hungry." The disciples asked, "How could we ever get enough bread in this deserted spot to satisfy such a crowd?" Then he directed the crowd to seat themselves on the ground. He took the seven loaves and fish, and after giving thanks he broke them and gave them to his disciples, who in turn gave them to the crowds. All ate until they were full.

Do our rational questions sometimes quench the miraculous power of God? Are we ready to respond radically to Jesus' call to leave all and follow him until we begin to think of more moderate ways to "spiritualize" his teaching? Is this really moderating and spiritualizing, or is it just compromising? If we radically and totally abandon everything and follow Jesus, God will provide for us. He healed and fed this multitude. Will he abandon the multitude who leave all to follow him today?   □

Faith Must Be Practiced
Matthew 7:21, 24-27 (Thursday, First Week Advent)

Anyone who hears my words and puts them into practice . . . (v. 24)

It is not enough to simply sit around and read the words of Jesus. We must live them! Many of us think that because we read the words of the gospel, or feel good when we read about Jesus, that we are born again or saved. But this is not enough!

The radical Christian is one who lives what he reads and who prays for what he lives. It is faith put into action. True, Paul says, "For it is by grace you have been saved, through faith—and this is not from yourselves, it is the gift of God—not by works, so that no one can boast." But James also says, "My brothers, what good is it to profess faith without practicing it? Such faith has no power to save one, has it? . . . You must perceive that a person is justified by his works and not by faith alone."

Again, James says, "A man who listens to God's word but does not put it into practice is like a man who looks into a mirror at the face he was born with; he looks at himself, then promptly goes off and forgets what he looked like. There is, on the other hand, the man who peers into freedom's ideal law and abides by it. He is no forgetful listener, but one who carries out the law in practice."

Francis of Assisi is thought to be a radical Christian—perhaps the most radical in all of history—because he was "no forgetful listener" of the gospel. He would hear the gospel and immediately go out and obey Jesus' commands. If the gospel said, "Sell what you have and give to the poor," Francis did it. If it said, "Preach to all creation," he began preaching.

Consequently, Francis was a very radical and spontaneous Christian.

Are we this radical, or do we let time soften the hard sayings of Jesus? In time we can figure out many ingenious ways to get around the challenges of Christ. Many times it is best to respond immediately. This is the way the apostles responded. It is the way Francis responded too. In many things Jesus wants an immediate response from us. In all things it must be without compromise. Such a one is "like the wise man who built his house on rock," the sure tested rock of God's word. ☐

Speak Out Your Faith
Matthew 9:27-31 (Friday, First Week Advent)

Are you confident I can do this? (v. 28)

Jesus asks this question of the two blind men before he heals them. They answer with an immediate "Yes, Lord." Jesus then touches them and says, "Because of your faith it shall be done to you."

How does such faith work? How do we have this confidence when all the natural world says that such healings are impossible? In a sense, we must become blind to the natural world of skepticism and doubt before we can be given true spiritual sight. In Mark's Gospel Jesus says we must have "no inner doubts but believe that what we say will happen. If you are ready to believe that you will receive whatever you ask for in prayer, it shall be done to you." Speaking our faith is, thus, very important.

In the Mid-Eastern world almost all prayer was verbal. Likewise, the monks of the early church prayed the scriptures by speaking the scriptures out loud, if only in a soft voice, throughout all the activities of their day. Thus, their lives were slowly conformed to the scriptures they spoke and prayed. True, Paul says to "Pray in the Spirit at all times" and "The

Spirit himself makes intercession for us with groanings that cannot be expressed in speech."

But he also says, "If you confess with your lips . . . you will be saved. Faith in the heart leads to justification, confession on the lips to salvation." Both Jesus and Paul see a real connection between the spoken words of the lips and the miraculous healing power of God in the world.

Perhaps this is because, "The mouth speaks whatever fills the mind" as Jesus says. And "Whatever you think, so will it be," says Proverbs. The thoughts that control our life overflow into our words, and our words give form and shape to our thoughts. Furthermore, "Death and life are in the power of the tongue." Thus the confidence that Jesus asks for in today's gospel can often be strengthened by speaking out our faith. And both life and death can be spoken into existence by the tongue.

Do we really use the power of our words constructively, or do we use our tongue in speaking negative thoughts about ourselves and others? Do we take the time to speak our faith in Jesus' action in our life every day? When we pray, do we really believe Jesus for what we ask, or do we have hidden doubts? Begin voicing your prayers out loud, whether with others or by yourself. Begin speaking your positive faith in Jesus and you will begin to see results. Then we will be healed of our blindness and see Jesus' miraculous working in our life! □

Let Yourself Be Evangelized
Matthew 9:35-10:1, 6-8 (Saturday, First Week Advent)

The harvest is good but laborers are scarce. Beg the harvest master to send out laborers to gather his harvest. (v. 37, 38)

Jesus calls us today to evangelize! The crowds of our day are exhausted from trying to live in the materialistic world. They are weary from trying to find their own way. They follow guru after guru and teacher after teacher. They read every new book to try and find relief. They fast, they diet, they think positively, yet they remain "like sheep without a shepherd."

The church has the good news everyone is looking for! We have the gospel of Jesus Christ. It out-mystifies the greatest mystic, and out-practices the greatest practitioner. In a way simple enough for a child it shares everything we need to know of the mysterious wisdom of God! We possess the wisdom of two thousand years of experiencing the reign of the Risen Christ, so we build confidently upon the experience of the past.

I believe that no other Christian sect or denomination possesses this wealth of both practical and mystical experience. No other group has had such an abundance of both success and failure from which to learn. The church possesses unequally the rich tradition of radical gospel living which spans every age, every time, every nation and culture. The Catholic church has much to share with the spiritually hungry people of today's world. We have Jesus, the Bread of Life!

Yet how can we share what we do not personally possess? Jesus says, "The gift you have received, give as a gift." Do we personally possess that which we publicly proclaim? Or do we try to experience Jesus vicariously through the experience of someone else? Francis says, "We ought to be ashamed of ourselves; we who are servants of God try to win honor and glory by recounting and making known what [the saints] have done." Likewise concerning scripture: "A man has been killed by the letter when he wants to know quotations only so that people will think he is very learned." It is not enough to know about the saints. We must be saints! It is not enough to know about scripture. We must live the scriptures! If we live the scripture we will be saints, and if we are saints of God we will bring people to God. The gospel must be experienced before it can be shared. This is a basic principle of evangelization.

Do we take time to experience Jesus before we try to share Jesus? Do we try to expound theories we have not yet lived? Such evangelization is vain. It will come to nothing. Take the time to get to know the real Jesus, then you can really help the people of Jesus. Let yourself be evangelized by Christ, then you can be a Christian evangelist. Share what you have received from Christ. Then you will find you have enough to feed even the multitudes! □

Empowered by the Spirit
Luke 5:17-26 (Monday, Second Week Advent)

The power of the Lord made him heal. (v. 17)

Such is the true healing from God. It is not something of man. It is from God. As Paul says of what he teaches, "I assure you, brothers, the gospel I proclaimed to you is no mere human invention."

This power is like a fire. It burns within the soul, destroying all that is not entirely of God and warming the coldness of a hardened human heart. When it is poured into the soul, it must bubble over. There is little choice about it. It simply happens when the power of God is poured into the vessel of the human soul.

Of this power Paul says, "Preaching the gospel is not the subject of a boast; I am under compulsion and have no choice. I am ruined if I do not preach it! I am . . . entrusted with a charge." Even with Paul, it was the "power of the Lord" which "made him" preach. Ministry of such power compels one to serve in the capacity given by God. With Francis, "His mouth spoke out of the abundance of his heart and the fountain of enlightened love that filled his whole being bubbled forth outwardly."

Paul writes to Timothy of the importance of this power: "Do not forget this: there will be terrible times in the last days. Men will . . . make a pretense of religion but negate its power." What is this power? Paul tells Timothy what it is not: "Men will be lovers of self and of money, proud, arrogant, abusive, disobedient to their parents, ungrateful, profane, inhuman, implacable, slanderous, licentious, brutal, hating the good . . . treacherous, reckless, pompous, lovers of pleasure . . . always learning but never able to reach a knowledge of the truth." How many of us are really innocent of any of these? As James says, "The man who has offended in one is guilty of all "

The western churches, in fact, often seem filled with people who do not know this power! We are a culture gone mad with the love of self and of money, so that even our Christianity must be prosperous in order to be recognized as blessed by God. Yet Jesus says, "Blessed are the poor." Never before has a culture enjoyed so much pleasure, yet the scriptures say, "Make no provision for the desires of the flesh." Both our church leaders and our laymen conduct themselves with the poise and confidence of the affluent which borders on pomp and arrogance. Following the poor Christ, we live ourselves like princes and kings! Never before has theology enjoyed such literary and scientific knowledge of the truth. Paul's list tells us clearly that even much of the Christianity of today does not yet know this power of God!

Yet Jesus promised this power to the church from the beginning! "Remain in Jerusalem until you are clothed with power from on high." What is this power? "Within a few days you will be baptized with the Holy Spirit," he said. As he promised, "Tongues as of fire appeared, which parted and came to rest on each of them. All were filled with the Holy Spirit. They began to express themselves in foreign tongues and to make bold proclamations as the Spirit prompted them."

Do we really know the power of the Spirit in our life? Has it come like a fire to burn away the hay and the stubble, or is our life still filled with the form of religion, which is powerless to rid us of hypocrisy, materialism, and sin? True religion is filled with power! It enables us to break free of the prisons of such vice. It enables us bring this healing freedom to all around us. In fact, if our life is empowered with the Spirit we are compelled, driven as by "a strong driving wind" to minister the healing love of Jesus Christ to all the earth! □

Suffering Comes Through Sin
Matthew 18:12-14 (Tuesday, Second Week Advent)

It is no part of your heavenly Father's plan that a single one of these little ones shall ever come to grief. (v. 14)

Poverty, sickness, death: where do they come from? They are not part of God's perfect plan. They were never willed into being by a God who, as Francis of Assisi exclaims, is "perfect good, all good, every good, the true and supreme good, and he alone is good!"

The scriptures have it that such things come from sin. As Paul says, "Through one man sin entered the world and with sin, death, death thus coming to all men inasmuch as all sinned." As James so poignantly says, "Once passion has conceived, it gives birth to sin, and when sin reaches maturity it begets death." Likewise, the Deuteronomic and Levitical law itself teaches that obedience brings blessing, but disobedience brings the curses of sickness, starvation, and war. Such things are not part of God's plan, and do not come from him. They come because of the sin of the whole human race!

These sins are obvious: nations oppress nations, governments oppress individuals, and individuals oppress the lowly. We are born into a world of pre-existing hatred and prejudice. We are born into a world already soiled by the stain of sin. But how do we respond to this fact of existence? Do we continue to accuse those who suffer of being guilty of some personal sin when so much of this world's sin is collective and corporate?

Jesus confronts such judgments when he says, "Do you think these were the greatest sinners just because they suffered this? By no means!" Such an attitude of self-righteous, condescending judgment is simply not acceptable according to the teaching of Jesus!

Today's gospel gives us the proper response: "What is your thought on this: a man owns a hundred sheep and one of them wanders away; will he not leave the ninety-nine out on the hills and go in search of the stray?" Jesus does not condemn the poor, the sick and the oppressed, he delivers them! He does not judge, he saves! We must leave our own security in order to bring God's security to the insecure.

Jesus describes and summarizes his own approach when he says to John's disciples, "Go and report to John what you have seen and heard. The blind recover their sight, cripples walk, lepers are cured, the deaf hear, dead men are raised to life, and the poor have the good news preached to them." Furthermore, Jesus is willing to actually become poor to save the poor, sick to save the sick, oppressed to save the oppressed! Paul says, "Christ has delivered us from the power of the law's curse by himself becoming a curse for us."

How do we respond to sin? Do we condemn or do we try to save? Do we judge or do we love? Do we become self-righteous and piously arrogant, or do we humble ourselves to help the lowly? Jesus became "like his brothers in every way.... Since he himself was tested through what he suffered, he was able to help those who are tempted." Are we willing to actually become like those we help? Are we willing to sacrifice in order to save? To become cursed to save the cursed? If not, our help cannot be accurately called Christian, or Christ-like. Paul says, "I could even wish to be separated from Christ for the sake of my brothers."

We must be on fire to relieve the suffering we see in this world. It is not of God! If we are of God we must work "to reconcile everything in Christ, both on earth and in the heavens, making peace through the blood of his cross." We cannot be passive about the poor if we follow Jesus. We cannot be non-caring about the shut-in and the sick. We cannot restrain our tears when we hear of death. We must respond, and we must respond today! We must respond from the depths of our heart. We must respond with our whole life. We must respond by giving our whole life so that at least one other life might be saved! This is the challenge of today's gospel. ☐

The Cross Is Freedom
Matthew 11:28-30 (Wednesday, Second Week Advent)

My yoke is easy and my burden light. (v. 30)

The cross of Jesus Christ is at once both heavy and light. First it seems to take away our natural freedom, then we find that it becomes a source of freedom! The cross of Jesus is indeed a great mystery, for in it the seeming contradictions of heaviness and lightness, slavery and freedom are reconciled as one.

When we first follow Jesus, it does seem as though all our freedom is taken away. We no longer are free to get drunk, to take drugs, or engage freely in many sexual relationships. Our old friends might even mock us: "You say you are free, but we are the ones who are really free." At first we might be left stammering and speechless in reply but deep down we know that they are not right.

True freedom is like a train on a track. The track seems to restrict the direction of the train, but without the track the train cannot reach either its full speed or its desired destination. In fact, when a train derails and goes off the track, it ends in destruction.

The track is like the guidance of God's truth. The train is like God's love. Love without truth might be well intentioned, but it will never acheive its goal. Love might seem to be restricted by God's truth, but it is only by the guidance of truth that love is really free to succeed. Some people say that God's only truth is love, but this is like saying a train can reach its destination without a track. It simply does not work.

The Book of Sirach speaks of the yoke of discipline in seeking the balance between God's love and God's truth as "wisdom." It says, "My son, from your youth embrace discipline, thus will you find wisdom with graying hair .... Put your feet into her fetters and your neck under her yoke. Stoop your shoulders and carry her. . . . Thus will you afterward find rest in her. . . . Her fetters will be your throne of majesty; her bonds, your purple cord." Here scripture affirms that if we limit our freedom by God's truth, this truth will support us in the long run as we seek to share and live in God's love.

The cross Jesus bore was indeed heavy. He fell under its weight on the way to Calvary. No doubt, its heaviness bruised his shoulder as he walked the via dolarosa, the "way of the cross." The cross was the instrument of his death. But it was also his support in death. It was his support in his final rest. It was on the cross that he totally abandoned his own strength and called out to the Father, "Into your hands I commend my spirit." It was because of this that the Father raised him from death to life. In this rest, he found eternal peace. In this death, Jesus was raised to life to sit forever at the right hand of the Father.

Paul says our new life in Christ begins with a similar death to our old self. He says, "Be intent on things above rather than on things of earth. After all, you have died. . . . Put to death whatever in your nature is rooted in earth; fornication, uncleanliness, passion, evil desires, and that lust which is idolatry. . . . Your conduct was once of this sort when these sins were your very life. You must put all that aside now: all the anger and quick temper, the malice, the insults, the foul language. . . . Put aside your old self with its past deeds and put on the new man."

Are we really ready to embrace the disciplines of God's truth in order to give full freedom to the love of God in our life? Or do we want one without the other? Do we conform God's truth to our life of sin, just because we don't want to go through the cross of dying to sin? I want to encourage you today. If you stoop your shoulders under the discipline of the cross of Christ, you will find a new life better and freer than you could ever imagine. If you embrace the cross and choose to crucify your old life of sin, God's truth and God's love will redirect your life and raise you up to greater heights than you ever thought possible. If you allow God's truth to direct your whole life, you will be able to give "full throttle" to God's power of love, and you will reach your desired destination with all the speed of the Spirit of God. □

Doing Violence to Our Violence
Matthew 11:11-15 (Thursday, Second Week Advent)

Until now the kingdom of God has suffered violence, and the violent take it by force. (v. 12)

True, Jesus is the Prince of Peace, but so often his words seem sharp and violent, cutting to the heart of the cancer of sin and darkness. True, Jesus speaks against violence, but he speaks with words as sharp as a two-edged sword. "Indeed, God's word is living and effective, sharper than any two edged sword." When Jesus comes again at the end of the world he will slay the nations of darkness with "the sword which comes out of his mouth." Even while on earth Jesus' words were often sharp and evoked immediate response to his gospel of peace. He says, "Do not suppose that my mission on earth is to spread peace. My mission is to spread, not peace, but division. . . . in short, to make a man's enemies those of his own household." The commitment Jesus demands is all or nothing. It does "violence" to all that is compromised!

Jesus encourages us to be forceful with ourselves as we battle our own tendency to sin. "If your right hand offends you, cut it off!" exclaims this Savior who is "meek and lowly of heart." Jesus minces no words when speaking about sin. He wastes no time! At the beginning of his ministry he proclaimed this theme: "Reform your lives! The kingdom of heaven is at hand!"

Jesus calls us to change, and to change now! He does not dilly-dally with the forces of darkness within. He wars against them!

Paul says, "Put on the armor of God so that you may be able

to stand against the tactics of the devil. Our battle is not against human forces, but against the principalities and powers, the rulers of this world of darkness, the evil spirits in regions above." He says our armor consists of truth, justice, zeal to propagate the gospel of peace, the shield of faith, the helmet of salvation and the sword of the Spirit, the word of God!

But Paul is also aware of a battle inside himself, a battle within his own eternal soul! "I cannot understand my own actions. I do not do what I want to do but what I hate . . . I see in my body's members a law at war with the law of my mind."

This inner struggle is common to all. It is usually overcome by readjusting our motivations so that they become motivations of the Spirit. Sometimes, however, they must be overcome by violence and brute force. This is why Jesus says "If your right hand offends you, cut it off!"

In this sense we must get violent and aggressive with ourselves as we strive to overcome sin. We must take to heart Paul's warnings about clear and straightforward sins in our life, habits and patterns: "These are the sins that bring down God's wrath." We must actively and zealously turn from these sins, or do penance and follow Jesus. As Francis says, "We humbly beg and implore everyone to persevere in the true faith and in a life of penance; there is no other way to be saved."

In today's gospel Jesus extols John the Baptist, who lived in the Spirit of Elijah the prophet. "I assure you, history has not known a man born of woman greater than John the Baptizer." John was violent with himself so he might be a worthy vessel to proclaim the coming of the gentle Lamb of God. Elijah himself was strident and caustic in his calls to penance as he prepared to find God in the "still, small voice." Both men knew this holy violence so they might prepare the way for peace.

Are we willing to do violence to the living darkness within us in order to fully crucify it, or do we let sin hang on in our life? If we let sin live, it will kill us, and only by killing sin will we freely live. Without this crucifixion there can be no life. Are we willing to put to death that which brings forth death within? Are we willing to do violence to our violence, so we might be a child of peace? Are we willing to prepare the way for the coming of the gentle Christ by getting tough with the brutality within?   □

Who Are the True Prophets?
Matthew 11:16-19 (Friday, Second Week Advent)

We piped you a tune but you did not dance! We sang you a dirge but you did not wail! (v. 17)

How true it is that we rarely accept the prophets who are sent to us. Jesus himself says, "I shall send you prophets and wise men and scribes. Some you will kill and crucify, others you will flog in your synagogues and hunt down from city to city."

Jesus never really promises us success. He only promises us that we will achieve what he achieved. "No pupil outranks his teacher, no slave his master. The pupil should be glad to become like his teacher, the slave like his master. If they call the head of the house Beelzebul, how much more the members of his household." They did not accept Jesus, nor will they accept his follower. Whatever success we enjoy will be temporary and short lived at best.

It is futile to hope that our peace movements or social justice campaigns will achieve lasting peace in this world. Jesus never promised they would.

This does not mean that we should fail to work for evangelism or for peace or social justice. Jesus says, "It must be that offenses come into the world, but woe to the person through whom the offenses come!" He tells us to work to spread the gospel. He warns us that he must find us working when he comes again!

Worse yet is the fact that most people will respond neither positively nor negatively, but with apathy. The worst response is no response. "For them you are only a ballad singer, with a pleasant voice and a clever touch. They listen to your words, but they will not obey them." Oh yes, we may even be popular on the religious circuit, but often it will be for all the wrong reasons. It is fashionable to talk about a radical Christian lifestyle, but such a lifestyle is seldom really lived. I ask myself as I am writing this book whether I will really live up to the words I write you.

Jesus says, "Woe to you when all speak well of you. Their fathers treated the false prophets in just this way." True, Jesus promises that we will do even "greater things" than he did, but he never uses worldly success or acceptance as the gauge for greatness. On the contrary, he says that such success is not a gauge for the prophet, but for the false prophet!

Can we really discern true prophecy from false prophecy? Are those we popularly accept as prophets really those Jesus Christ sends to prepare his way, or has our worldliness and commercialism so clouded our spiritual view that we can barely discern the will of God anymore? Worse yet, are we the false prophets? Let us break totally free of the external judgments of success or failure, and judge only according to the will of God. Let us hear his word and obey. Let us accept the prophecy that comes through both the popular and the unpopular. Yet, let us accept only the prophetic message which is the authentic gospel. Then will we dance to the divine melody of Jesus Christ! Then will our life itself become his prophet's song. □

The Kingdom Is Coming
Matthew 17:10-13 (Saturday, Second Week Advent)

Elijah has already come, but they did not recognize him and they did as they pleased with him. (v. 12)

Elijah has come! He has "restored everything." Then why has so little changed? Where is the promised Messiah? Where is the kingdom of peace, the restoration of justice, the reign of God?

The coming of these things is not so much a matter of a change in the world as it is a change in our heart. Kingdoms only change when men change, and men only change when hearts are converted. Once the Messiah comes to our soul then, and only then, will we discover the reign of God in this world. If we find his peace in our soul, then we will suddenly discover an abundance of peace even in the midst of a war torn world, comfort even in the midst of pain, and eternal life even in the midst of death.

The reign of God is incarnated within this human world and the human world is transubstantiated into the kingdom of God. Even as Jesus is found under the appearance of the humblest and tiniest morsels of bread and a small cup of wine, so also is he found within even the most humble and mundane people and circumstances in our life. Spiritual joy is incarnated within sorrow so that sorrow itself is transubstantiated into the joy of the Christ child! Without the eyes of faith the natural world remains mundane and dreary, but with the eyes of faith all the world is daily renewed in the supernatural miracle of Christ! Without the eyes of faith we cannot perceive the miracle!

This is what Jesus speaks of today. Without the faith that comes from God, the religious leaders of his day were unable to see the Spirit of Elijah within John the Baptist. Oh, I am not talking about some far-out theory of reincarnation that is to be understood only with theology and complicated speculation. I am talking about a continuing incarnation of the fiery Spirit of prophecy that was given both to Elijah and to John and is burned into the soul of all who believe. This is the Spirit of wisdom who "is the refulgence of eternal light, the spotless mirror of the power of God, the image of his goodness" who "passes into holy souls from age to age, and produces friends of God and prophets." Such was the Spirit who passed into both Elijah and into John.

Do we recognize this prophetic Spirit today? She still passes into holy souls. Do we still fail to recognize her? Do we recognize the prophets in our midst? They are with us still. "Today is the day of salvation. If today you hear his voice harden not your heart." Do our hardened hearts cloud our eyes and blind us to the miracles of faith?

Know, too, that the day of Jesus' coming is closer than it was even a moment ago. "The day of salvation is closer than the hour we first believed." Both Elijah and John the Baptist call out more than ever to "Prepare the way of the Lord!" Let us open our ears to their constant prophetic cry and respond with John, "Amen! Come, Lord Jesus!" □

Jesus Begins a New Priesthood
Matthew 21:23-27 (Monday, Third Week Advent)

On what authority are you doing these things? Who has given you this power? (v. 23)

It must be clearly understood that Jesus had no established authority within Judaism. Nor did John the Baptist. They were neither priests nor recognized members of any religious sect or community. At best they were perpetual Nazarites, but this was an ancient rite open to any individual who sought to faithfully fulfill the vow. To be a Nazarite did not constitute membership in a community or ordination to preach and teach.

Yet both John the Baptist and Jesus taught multitudes. They taught in synagogues or in the open wilderness, and the people listened! Jesus even had the audacity to preach in the precincts of the temple at Jerusalem. This is what so upset the chief priests and elders of the people in today's gospel.

Furthermore, there was the problem of baptism. Where is baptism mentioned in the law? You will find it nowhere! You will find circumcision. You will find various private vows. You will find priestly consecration. But you will not find any mention of baptism. What did it signify? Wasn't the commitment already mentioned in the law good enough for these new zealots and self-styled prophets? How dare they go beyond the law and step outside the authority already established.

Jesus was both conservative and progressive! He said, "Do not think that I have come to abolish the law and the prophets. I have come, not to abolish them, but to fulfill them." He also said, "The scribes and the Pharisees have succeeded Moses as teachers; therefore, do everything and observe everything they tell you." Jesus also supported the new, non-scriptural practice of baptism, established new religious rites for his disciples by giving new meaning to the Passover through the Lord's Supper, and taught with the authority of a rabbi, even though we have no evidence that he was either schooled or ordained.

From the comfortable perspective of 2,000 years it is rather easy to say that Jesus, as God incarnate, was establishing the new covenant spoken of by the prophets. Therefore, there would be a change in both the priesthood and the ritual, for the new covenant would include not just the Jews, but all the peoples of the earth. The Book of Hebrews speaks eloquently of this change, and Christian theologians have nicely and neatly explained it so that it all seems quite normal and proper.

But think of the perspective of people in Jesus' and John's own day! What faith! What total and trusting openness to the Spirit they possessed. What simple perception into divine mystery they were given to be able to accept the priesthood of Jesus, "established according to the order of Melchizedek." This is not a priesthood that can be perceived by any objective lineage or visible ordination by the laying on of hands. This is a priesthood of the Spirit established by the mysterious hands of the King of Salem, who was "without father, mother or ancestry, without beginning of days or end of life, like the Son of God he remains a priest forever."

The challenge remains for us to be open to this authority of the Spirit within the legitimate apostolic authority of the church today. In the early church this was done. As the *Didache* says, "Let the prophets celebrate the Eucharist as much as they please." No doubt this led to confusion so that eventually only ordained clerics were allowed to preside at the altar. We must, however, continue to find ways to manifest the royal priesthood of the whole people enlivened by the Spirit! We must recognize that, even today, a mystical priesthood after the "order of Melchizedek" is conferred on those who literally and radically imitate and follow Jesus Christ, the only great High Priest. It is within the legitimate authority of the church, but it is also without and beyond it. God cannot be controlled by man!

Are we open to an authority we cannot categorize and institutionalize, or are we uncomfortable with a divine authority we cannot humanly control? Jesus would not directly answer the question put to him in today's gospel. He answered only with another question about such divine authority. The chief priests and elders of the people could not answer him. Could you answer him today? ☐

It Is Not Too Late to Change
Matthew 21:28-32 (Tuesday, Third Week Advent)

There was a man who had two sons. He approached the elder and said, "Son, go out and work in the vineyard today." The son replied, "I am on my way, sir"; but he never went. Then the man came to his second son and said the same thing. This son said in reply, "No, I will not"; but afterward he regretted it and went. Which of the two did what the father wanted? (v. 28-31)

How many of us really do what our heavenly Father wants? How many of us actually do radical things for Jesus? Jesus says, "The harvest is rich but the workers are few." How many of us respond willingly to the call of Christ and then end up doing nothing?

But do not despair! The message of today's gospel is

repentance. It is a message of hope. Even if you have spoken against God and refused the call of Jesus, today you can still turn back and faithfully respond to his call for you.

Often it is those we expect the least of who serve God most faithfully in the long run. Those who go to seminaries often deny him, even though they study about him every day. Even those who shepherd his flock as priests, deacons and bishops often deny him in their personal lives. Many times the uneducated and the simple and the poor serve him most perfectly. Francis tells us "It is easier to ascend to heaven from a hovel than from a palace." Paul says, "Not many of you are wise . . . not many are influential, and surely not many are well born." Jesus says, "I assure you that tax collectors and prostitutes are entering the kingdom of God before you."

That is why God worked so frequently with the simple when he did his greatest miracles on earth. Peter was a fisherman. So were the other apostles. Mary was but a poor and simple maiden when she bore the Son of God.

Those who were educated were usually great sinners. Paul killed Christians in the name of the justice of God. Augustine lived a life of revelry and sexual immorality.

Yet, in repentance all are made equal, for all are sinners in the eyes of God. The educated and religious Saul of Tarsus was no better than Peter the fisherman. Augustine, the scholar, was no better than Francis, the "idiot." Even Mary, were it not for the grace of God, would have been a sinner like us if left to her own efforts. By her own merit she is no better than the worst of sinners, but by the grace of God she has become a model of sinlessness for all believers. She has become the perfect model of the church. She was all the more humble for having been chosen by God as a spotless bride to bear the sinless Son of God who would take away the sins of the world.

Are we a people of penance? Are we always ready to repent? Or do we speak bold words for God and then do little to change our lives? Our life must change if our words are to mean anything before God. We must not only say we will labor in the spiritual vineyard, we must labor as we proclaim. Then our works will bring forth the fruit of the Spirit. Otherwise, both our words and our works will be fruitless and vain in the harvest of God. But be encouraged by the gospel today. Repent and change. It is not too late to really follow God today. □

No Miracles without Compassion
Luke 7:18-23 (Wednesday, Third Week Advent)

The blind recover their sight, cripples walk, lepers are cured, the deaf hear, dead men are raised to life, and the poor have the good news preached to them. Blest is that man who finds no stumbling block in me. (v. 22-23)

Do we accept the full ministry and witness of Jesus, or do we only accept it in part? Many who work for the poor through social justice programs do not really accept the more charismatic dimension to life in Christ. Likewise, many charismatics neglect the social dimension of the gospel which is to be preached specifically to the poor.

The charismatic dimension was a definite experience of the early church. The descent of the Holy Spirit was accompanied with "tongues as of fire." After this many wonders and signs were performed by the apostles. Among the list of ministries in the early church, Paul lists "miracle workers, healers, and those who speak in tongues." The words of Peter to the cripple must have expressed a common experience among the first believers: "I have neither silver nor gold, but what I have I give to you! In the name of Jesus Christ, the Nazarene, walk!" Jesus did commission the apostles to cure the sick, raise the dead, heal the leprous, and expel demons.

To exercise this ministry involves great interior faith. Jesus says, "Put your trust in God. I solemnly assure you, whoever says to this mountain 'Be lifted up and thrown into the sea,' and has no inner doubts but believes that what he says will happen, shall have it done for him." Jesus worked miracles on the face of the earth and empowers us to do the same.

But none of this can be accomplished without a deep compassion for the poor. Jesus cured because of both faith and love. Faith without love is impersonal and cold. Love without faith is powerless and weak. It is misguided and incomplete at best.

If our miracles are to be truly Christian, they must be "like Christ." How did Jesus ultimately heal the world of sin? He did so by taking on the sins of the whole world personally. If we heal someone who is sick, our action is only fully Christian if we are willing to take on their sickness ourselves. If we feed them, we must be willing even to take on their hunger.

Paul tells us to both rejoice with those who rejoice, and to weep with those who weep. In his great love for the Israelites, he goes so far as to say, "I could even wish to be separated from Christ for the sake of my brothers, my kinsmen, the Israelites." For the church he says, "In my own flesh I fill up what is lacking in the sufferings of Christ for the sake of his body, the church."

Of course, God did not require Paul to go to hell so the Israelites could go to heaven, nor is the "once and for all" sacrifice of Christ on the cross incomplete so as to require a further atoning sacrifice from us to forgive others' sins. But mystically such a willingness on the part of Paul is the only proper response from one who seeks to literally follow the footsteps of Jesus and become a co-heir with the Lamb of God who takes away the sins of the world.

For many, the real Jesus is just a bit much. We are all in favor of love, but we would rather emphasize "love of self" than Jesus' straightforward statement that "Unless you lose your life for my sake you will never find it." Self-awareness is acceptable. Self-sacrifice scares us to death. Jesus is fine as long as he remains some new age guru who's gospel message is interpreted by means of self-awareness techniques or the latest spiritual fad. When Jesus becomes the stark and demanding

Jesus of scripture we cannot accept him. Then his teachings become the teachings of a fool. As Paul says, "We preach Christ crucified—a stumbling block to the Jews and an absurdity to the Gentiles." Do we find a stumbling block in the foolishness of the ministry of Christ?

Are we really willing to make such sacrifices for the salvation of the world? Do we really understand the charismatic mystery of Jesus' selfless love? Or is our work with the poor something so rational and logical that we have all but moved Jesus from the center of our work with the poor and afflicted of this world? Such Christian social work is powerless and limp. It puts band-aid after band-aid on the open sore of a mortal wound which can only be healed supernaturally. Jesus is the only Great Physician who can heal the wounds of the world. Do we really believe that he can work such a miracle? Jesus says, "Seek and you shall find. . . . ask and you will receive." James says, "You do not receive because you do not ask." Let us ask for the promised miracles of Jesus. Then we will really bring good news to the poor. □

We Are Desert People
Luke 7:24-30 (Thursday, Third Week Advent)

What did you go out to see in the desert. . . . someone dressed luxuriously? Remember, those who dress in luxury and eat in splendor are to be found in royal palaces. (v. 24-25)

The people of the church are desert people. We are in the world, but not of it. We must come out of Babylon and Egypt and venture into the desert if we are to find God on the Mount Sinais and Mount Horebs of our life. After baptism, we must go with Jesus into the desert before we can begin any successful ministry to the world. With Paul, we must sojourn in the solitary desert of Arabia before we openly preach to the whole world. As in today's gospel, we must go out into the desert of repentance before we can really receive Jesus into our life.

But the desert is not just a romantic notion you read about in spiritual books. The ascetic experiences of the desert fathers, the monks, and hermits of the early church, always seem quite edifying and even quaint when read about in the warm security of our homes. The experiences of an Antony or a Francis seem quite inspiring when read about while resting in a cozy, overstuffed chair by a warm fire, or before drifting off to sleep in a comfortable king size bed. But the actual experience of the saints would be unbearable for most of us, and tolerable for only a few.

The same holds true of the saints that live among us today. The example of Mother Teresa of Calcutta is a great inspiration. But how many would still find her inspiring after they shared her life? Could they endure her poverty, her fasting, her long hours of prayer? The concept of poverty we find appealing, but the actual touch of the poor we find obnoxious and nauseating. Could we endure her obedience to the church and her community discipline? I am afraid that most of us could not.

For us, such holiness remains a dream. We march for the poor, but refuse to become poor. We read books about prayer, but seldom pray. We go to charismatic gatherings, but refuse to really let the Spirit of God have full control of our lives. For us, such holiness remains only a pious illusion, an unattainable dream.

The only way to break through this illusion into real piety is to become radical. The message of Mary at Medjugorje exhorts all, but especially those of us who live in the West, to repent and to fast. This fasting breaks us free from the chains of our culture's materialism and immorality. It breaks us free from the very things we think we cannot do without.

Francis also had to make a radical break in his own day. For him it meant embracing the leper, or begging with the beggar. The very sight of lepers was nauseating to him and filled his soul with fear. What if he were to contract this awful disease? He realized that the only way to overcome his fear was to actually reach out and embrace the lepers. Likewise, the contents of his beggar's bowl made him want to vomit, but after he tasted it, even this became sweet to him.

Are we willing to go out into the deserts of our soul in order to be prepared for the coming of Christ? Are we willing to reach out and embrace the rough reality of the lepers and the beggars we find in the deserts of our own culture? In the desert we will fast, but we will be freed of our gluttonous craving for fine food. We will wear a rough garment of camel's hair, but we will be freed of our preoccupation with passing style and faddish trends. No doubt, we will get lonely, but we will be free from the misguided intimacy of sexual immorality. We will touch the desert sun, and our skin will burn, but at least we will know that this desert is no illusion, no spiritual mirage. Do we seek to be clothed with the reality of the desert, or do we prefer the comfort of a royal palace? This is the question of today's gospel. □

Two Kinds of Fire
John 5:33-36 (Friday, Third Week Advent)

He was the lamp, set aflame and burning bright. . . . Yet I have a testimony greater than John's, namely, the works the Father has given me to accomplish. These very works which I perform testify on my behalf that the Father has sent me. (v. 35-36)

We, too, are to give witness to Jesus Christ. But this witness is not something we are to give only with words. We are to witness with our whole life. Words without a changed life are empty and unconvincing, yet a changed life speaks with clarity even without words.

Jesus says, "In [the Messiah's] name, penance for the remission of sins is to be preached to all the nations, beginning at Jerusalem. You are witnesses of this." But he also says, "Your light must shine before men so that they may see goodness in your acts and give praise to your heavenly Father."

John the Baptist said to the Pharisees and Sadducees who came to be baptized, "You brood of vipers! Who told you to flee from the wrath to come! Give some evidence that you meant to reform. . . . Even now the ax is laid to the root of the tree. Every tree that is not fruitful will be cut down and thrown into the fire." Their works had to become inflamed by God so they would not be destroyed by fire.

Two kinds of fire are spoken of. One brings light. Another brings judgment. John is "set aflame and burning bright" as he speaks of both. He baptizes with water, but tells of a baptism with fire which is fulfilled both by the outpouring of the Spirit with tongues of fire at Pentecost and by the burning chaff with "unquenchable fire" at the last judgment. Ironically, the fire seems to be the same. The way we receive it into our life makes the difference.

Jesus says, "I have come to light a fire on the earth. How I wish the blaze were ignited! I have a baptism to receive. What anguish I feel till it is over." This baptism of fire was the cross.

In the cross the fire of judgment and the fire of the Spirit become one. All that differs is the attitude in which we accept it. For some, the fire of the cross is a way to make them strong. For others, it is judgment. True, on the cross Jesus bore the judgment of all the world, but the cross was also the means for bringing resurrection to all. True, the fire of God burns away our "wood, hay and straw" when it is embraced, but it also purifies our "precious stones" like "fire tried silver or gold."

Some long to embrace the fire like a lover. Others are afraid of the fire and spend their life avoiding it like a curse. Others embrace it with passion. Others run from it with terror. The cross is this place of passion. It is the place of love. It is the place of a judgment which brings both purification and forgiveness. Our works can only be light if they are first fire. Jesus says we are the light of the world because we are first "lamps." Our works must be inflamed by both the Spirit and the cross if they are to give light to the world. They must be set on fire. "Fire will test the quality of each man's work," says Paul. Let us become one with the fire of God, so our works will shine before all the world as lamps.

Are our works on fire for God? Have we allowed ourselves to pass through the fire of the cross so we might know the shining glory of the resurrection? Do our works give witness to the Spirit of Christ within us, or do they betray our inner coldness and the spirit of the world? Today let us "stir into flame the gift of God" which has been given us. Let us be on fire. Let our works give witness to the very truth of Jesus Christ. □

Jesus' Family History
Matthew 1:1-17 (December 17)

A family record of Jesus Christ, son of David, son of Abraham. (v. 1)

Jesus might only have claimed priestly authority "after the order of Melchizedek," but his genealogy firmly established him in the Davidic line of kingship. It was from this line that the promised Messiah was expected to come.

God made a covenant with David that was eternal, "Your house and your kingdom shall endure forever before me; your throne shall stand firm forever." He also made a covenant with Abraham, "I will make your descendants as countless as the stars of the sky and the sands of the seashore. All the nations shall be blessed in you." Jesus stands as a Jew among Jews, as a son of Abraham, and a king among kings, as a son of David!

Yet this lineage is not so spotless as it might first seem. It is a lineage of real people who followed a real God in a real world. As such it is filled with people who were both saints and sinners. It includes both men and women. It includes both Jews and Gentiles. Even though the purity of the Davidic line of the Jewish king is established, it does not sidestep the real sins and flaws of the saints it includes. Rahab was a harlot. Ruth was a Moabite, a non-Jew. The wife of Uriah had committed adultery with David. The men mentioned in the genealogy are both great and petty, saints and sinners: usually both at once!

Even in the genealogy the universal mission of salvation undertaken by Jesus is proclaimed. In an environment of a religion exclusively for Jews, the faithful Moabite is mentioned. In a religious culture where male dominance is the norm, women of faith are mentioned. In a religion preoccupied with minute and detailed ritual purity, a faithful harlot is mentioned. In a lineage which is strongly Davidic, David's sin is not passed over in silence. As Paul says of Jesus' followers, "There does not exist among you Jew or Greek, slave or freeman, male or female. All are one in Christ Jesus."

This is because of the universal need for salvation. All are sinners, so all are equally in need of God's mercy. A person's family tree will not save them if they are living in sin. "Not all Israelites are true Israelites, and not all Abraham's descendants are his children. . . . It is not the children of the flesh who are children of God." As Paul also says, "All men have sinned and fallen short of the glory of God. All are now undeservedly justified by the gift of God through the redemption wrought in Christ Jesus. . . . God has imprisoned all in disobedience that he might have mercy on all." "It is the children of the promise who are descendants."

Are we really open to this universal mission, or do we also place external limits on the mysticism of the gospel? Respecting the authority of what has come before are we willing to step into the unknown of the future? Do we really appreciate the inner faith of all people, or do we judge them only according to externals?

The mission of Jesus is universal. Isaiah said, "In days to come the mountain of the Lord's house shall be established as the highest mountain and raised above the hills. All nations shall stream toward it; many peoples shall come and say: 'Come let us climb the Lord's mountain, to the house of the God of Jacob. That he may instruct us in his ways, and we may walk in his paths.'" Isaiah also said of them, "Not by appearance shall he judge, nor by hearsay shall he decide a right for the land's afflicted."

Today we are challenged to expand our universal gospel vision toward the future. If we can really come to appreciate even the lineage of Jesus' birth, we will come to gain new appreciation of his life, death and resurrection. As Francis said, "Let us now begin, for up until now we have done nothing." Let us examine these beginnings so we might properly meet the universal challenge of the future! □

Let the Spirit Conceive
Matthew 1:18-24 (December 18)

She was found with child through the power of the Holy Spirit. (v. 18)

How different is the sexuality of the secular world! Paul says, "It is obvious what proceeds from the flesh: lewd conduct, impurity... drunkenness, orgies and the like." In his Letter to the Romans he says, "Let us live honorably as in daylight; not in carousing and drunkenness, not in sexual excess and lust." To the Ephesians: "As for lewd conduct or promiscuousness or lust of any sort, let them not even be mentioned among you. Make no mistake about this: no fornicator, no unclean or lustful person in effect an idolator— has any inheritance in the kingdom of Christ and of God."

It is not that sexuality is bad. Hebrews says, "Let marriage be honored in every way and the marriage bed be kept undefiled." Paul says, "Every man should have his own wife and every woman her own husband. The husband should fulfill his conjugal obligations towards his wife, the wife towards her husband. . . . Do not deprive one another, unless by mutual consent for a time, to devote yourselves to prayer. Then return to one another, that Satan may not tempt you through your lack of self-control." In his letter to Timothy he warns, "The Spirit distinctly says that in later times some will turn away from the faith and will heed deceitful spirits and things taught by demons through plausible liars who forbid marriage."

It is clear that sex is good when used and enjoyed according to God's plan. Again Paul says, "Everything God created is good; nothing is to be rejected when it is received with thanksgiving, for it is made holy by God's word and by prayer." Jesus himself said of a man and woman joined in marriage, "Thus they are no longer two but one flesh. Therefore, let no man separate what God has joined." Likewise, he blessed the institution of marriage by performing his first miracle during his presence at the marriage at Cana.

Why is it, then, that the sexuality of the world is so strongly condemned in the scriptures? After all, wasn't polygamy practiced by the saints of the old covenant, as well as the common practice of keeping many concubines? It seems that men could lead a very fine sexual life as long as they could afford to support their wives and children!

Jesus says, "Anyone who looks lustfully at a woman has already committed adultery with her in his thoughts." Paul says, "Put to death whatever in your nature is rooted in earth; fornication, uncleanliness, passion, evil desires, and that lust which is idolatry." James says, "Once passion has conceived, it gives birth to sin, and when sin reaches maturity it begets death." Paul continues, "You must no longer live as the pagans do—their minds empty, their understanding darkened. They have abandoned themselves to lust and the indulgence of every sort of lewd conduct. This old self deteriorates through illusion and desire."

It is the lust which accompanies sexuality that is bad. Lust and misdirected passion start out as small sparks but grow into a flame that will consume a person. This passion will so consume that it will occupy one's every thought and desire. It will take precedence over God! Such passions and lust will eventually enslave us to it. That is why this lust is called idolatry by Paul, and why passion is the beginning of death according to James.

Mary stands as a symbol of a totally Spirit-controlled sexuality. By her chastity and virginity she says that we are called beyond the mere animal lust of human nature to a more divine passion in Christ. If we say yes to our divine Lover, then, with Mary, we will give birth to the Christ child in our life. We will bear the fruit of the Spirit spoken of by Paul: "Love, joy, peace, patient endurance, kindness, generosity, faith, mildness and chastity. Against such there is no law! Those who belong to Christ Jesus have crucified their flesh with its passions and desires. Since we live by the Spirit, let us follow the Spirit's lead!"

This is all fine and good. But how do we free ourselves from such passion and lust? Jesus says, "If your right eye is your trouble, gouge it out and throw it away! If your right hand is your trouble, cut it off and throw it away! Better to lose part of your body than to have it all cast into Gehenna." We are to take aggressive action against our temptations to lust and passion.

In his letter to the Colossians, Paul treats this subject of vice and virtue concluding, "Dedicate yourselves to thankfulness." The Psalms say, "Enter his courts with songs of praise and thanksgiving." Mary, herself, manifests the power of the Spirit within her by singing a song of praise: "My soul proclaims the greatness of the Lord." It is through praise and thanksgiving that we stir up the Spirit, and it is through the fire of the Spirit that we overcome the fire of sinful passion and lust.

Do we prefer the impregnation of the Holy Spirit over the sexuality of the world? Do we fill our mind with the illusions of lust and passion, or do we occupy our mind with thanksgiving and praise? Does our life manifest the fruit of the Spirit, or have we given in to practices of sexual impurity, excess, and lust? When this passion conceives it brings forth sin and begets death. When the Spirit conceives, the love of Jesus will daily burn anew in our life. □

Reflections on the Gospels · 145

Like Peter or Like Judas?
Luke 1:5-25 (December 19)

But now you will be mute—unable to speak—until the day these things take place, because you have not trusted my words. (v. 20)

The scriptures often show how different people respond to the same message in different ways. The same word of salvation is announced to all. It is our response to that word which makes the difference.

I suppose the most obvious example would be Peter and Judas. Both sinned. Both denied Jesus. Yet one responded with repentance that led to salvation, and the other responded in despair which led to his own damnation. One became the rock on which Jesus built his church. The other became the symbol for all traitors and sons of perdition throughout the ages. One was exalted on the throne of the kingdom of Christ on earth. The other hung upon a tree so that his bowels gushed forth with the blood money he cast into a potter's field. Both sinned; it was their response which made the difference.

Today's gospel offers a similar contrast in response to the word of God. On one side is Mary. On the other is Zechariah. Both responded with initial fear. Both asked the question "How can this be?" Yet deep within, there was a difference so that from one this was a question of childlike faith, while from the other it was a question of cynicism and doubt. One is looked upon as the model for faithfulness for all generations. The other is struck dumb by the angel because he did not trust. They both heard the same word of salvation. They both responded with the same question. Yet there was a different attitude within their heart. One believed, the other doubted. This made all the difference!

Yet there is also a major difference between Zechariah and Judas. Zechariah was "just in the eyes of God, blamelessly following all the commandments and ordinances of the Lord." Judas was a "son of perdition." Judas was lost for all eternity. Zechariah continues in the service of the Lord. Both are punished by God. But for one it is the punishment of eternal torment, while for the other it is the temporary chastisement of a loving God. For one the punishment is God's wrath, for another it is God's love. Again, both are punished. It is the attitude of the one who received the punishment that is different. One remains faithful. The other denies Christ in despair.

The scriptures speak of a loving chastisement from God. "My sons, do not disdain the discipline of the Lord, nor lose heart when he reproves you; for whom the Lord loves, he disciplines. . . . If you do not know the discipline of sons, you are not sons but bastards. We respected our earthly fathers who corrected us. . . . They disciplined us as seemed right to them, to prepare us for the short span of mortal life; but God does so for our true profit, that we may share his holiness."

This does not mean God doesn't forgive us our sins. He sometimes lets us experience the just consequence of our sins to show to us the result of sin. This is done to encourage us to follow righteousness. As the psalmist says, "For them I am a God who forgives, yet I punished all their offenses." Or as Paul writes of the incestuous believer, "I hand him over to Satan for the destruction of his flesh, so that his spirit may be saved on the day of the Lord."

This is not bad news. It is good news! God loves us enough to correct us in the flesh so that our spirits may prosper! If we wander too far to the right, or the left, he will guide us back to center with a firm but gentle hand. If our actions are sinful, he will let us see their consequence to show us again that he is really there and that he cares. He does not disappear in the dark. He is always with us. He is concerned for every part of our life. If we fall, his hand will raise us up again. If we sin, he will correct us so that he can do great things through us!

Do we really believe God can still do great things through us even though we sometimes backslide and sin? Do we see God's chastisement as wrathful or loving? Do we thank God for showing us his concern for every part of our life when he allows us to see the consequences of our own sin? Today we must choose. We are either to be like Peter or like Judas, like Mary or like Zechariah. Most of us will never be as perfect as Mary or as sinful as Judas. Most of us are like Zechariah. Let us follow his example and remain faithful to God, even though we sometimes sin and are chastised by the Lord. Then, as with Zechariah, God will still work miracles and wonders through our life to bring salvation to all the earth!   □

Fear of God
Luke 1:26-38 (December 20)

I am the servant of the Lord. Let it be done to me as you say. (v. 38)

Yesterday we saw the imperfect response of Zechariah. Today we see the perfect response of Mary.

Mary responds initially with fear. "She was deeply troubled by the angel's words, and wondered what his meaning meant." Gabriel responds, "Do not fear, Mary. You have found favor with God." The scriptures say two things about fear: "The fear of the Lord is the beginning of knowledge" and "Perfect love casts out all fear." Fear can be both compelling and crippling. Somewhere between these two extremes is wisdom. In all the infancy narratives the servants of God respond with an awe-filled fear. In all the accounts the angel of the Lord says, "Be not afraid." Jesus himself encourages his disciples to "Be not afraid" many times. We should know the fear of God which brings us to God's love, but once we know this love, all crippling fear is gone. We believe all things in this love.

Mary also questions: "How can this be since I do not know man?" Zechariah questions and it is counted to him as doubt. Mary questions and it is counted as faith. The psalmist says, "I pondered and my spirit questioned." It is alright to question God and to ponder as long as it is done in faith rather than doubt. An obedient child questions its parents in good faith, believing it will receive a helpful answer. A rebellious child questions in order to challenge a parent's authority and knowledge. Both question. Yet one is obedient and faithful while the other is rebellious and full of doubt. Mary questioned, but she never lost faith. No doubt, she continued to be filled with awe and wonder as she witnessed the great things God was doing through her Son!

Paul even speaks of a godly doubt when he says: "This treasure we possess in earthen vessels, to make it clear that its surpassing power comes from God and not from us. We are afflicted in every way possible, but we are not crushed; full of doubts, we never despair.... We do not lose heart, because our inner being is renewed each day even though our body is being destroyed at the same time." Here, then, is the key. To question, to fear, even to doubt, yet without losing our faith. Never to lose heart because the physical world seems to contradict the promises given by the Spirit. To know that while the natural world says some things are impossible, "with God all things are possible."

How do we question God? Do we question with doubt, or do we question in faith? Are we afraid of God, or does fear of God lead us to his love? Are we so scrupulous and paranoid that our spiritual life is crippled, or has a healthy fear compelled us to walk on in love? There is a big difference between being afraid of God, and possessing the fear of God which leads to wisdom. If we fear God, we will discover his love which casts out all fear. If we question God, we will find wisdom. Sometimes we are full of doubts, yet we will journey towards faith without despair. ☐

Jesus, Child in the Womb
Luke 1:39-45 (December 21)

When Elizabeth heard Mary's greeting, the baby leapt in her womb. Elizabeth was filled with the Holy Spirit and cried out in a loud voice: "Blest are you among women and blest is the fruit of your womb." (v. 41-42)

What a beautiful symbol we have in this gospel. It is through Mary's visit and greeting that Elizabeth is led to Jesus. It is with Mary's greeting that Elizabeth cries out in praise.

Notice that Elizabeth also responds to John. John is "filled with the Holy Spirit from his mother's womb" and helps his own mother to be filled with the Spirit. Likewise, it is the Spirit-filled babe in the womb who first responds to the Spirit-filled greeting of Mary, the mother of Jesus, who is the Son of God. It is a mere child of the womb who first responds to the one who bears the Christ child within her womb, and thus comes to bring the Holy Spirit to his own mother. Child responds to child, and both mothers are blest indeed! A mother responds in obedience and a child is born to bring a disobedient world to salvation.

Both Mary and Jesus are praised, but why? Mary is "the mother of my Lord." She is the *Theotokos*, the God-bearer. Just as the ark of the covenant was honored and reverenced because of the tablets of the law within, so too is Mary honored because of the Living Word she bore within her womb. Jesus is truly the "fruit of your womb."

Likewise, Mary is the model of faith. "Blest is she who trusted that the Lord's words to her would be fulfilled." She did not doubt like Zechariah. She trusted. She is, therefore, "blest among women." But not only is she blest among women. She is blest by all generations! "All ages to come shall call me blessed" proclaims the virgin in her hymn of praise. She is the model of faith for all.

What does all this say about the abortion issue today? John is filled with the Spirit "from his mother's womb." Jesus is called "blessed" even in Mary's womb. Jesus is called "Lord" even while still in Mary's womb. Even the fetal babe of John the Baptist responds to the fetal presence of Jesus within Mary's womb! Fetus calls to fetus, and both of the mothers are saved!

How can we possibly consider aborting a fetus within the womb, when the Holy Spirit so clearly dwelt within the fetus of John the Baptist? How can we treat life so cheaply, when Jesus has sanctified the fetal state by being declared both "blessed" and "Lord" while he himself was in the womb? Abortion is not only the taking of life, it is an irreverence towards Jesus, the Lord, and Author of life. It is not only a taking of physical human life, it is denying the Holy Spirit! How can we deny such a child the opportunity of hearing the good news in life when it was just such a child who brought forth the good news of life even to its mother from the womb!

Can we hear the greeting of Mary today? Do we recognize the Christ child within her? Do we really call Mary blessed, or do we only passively recognize her role in the birth of Christ? Does our recognition of the blessedness of Mary, the *Theotokos,* stir up the Spirit within the womb of our own life? Do we see the beauty of their connection? If we want to know the Spirit of Jesus more, look more to Mary. If we want to experience more of the salvation of the child, look more to his mother. If we want to bring salvation to the mature and wise of the world, let us first attend to God's Living Word within the Virgin Mother's womb!   □

The Mirror of God
Luke 1:46-56 (December 22)

My being proclaims the greatness of the Lord. (v. 46)

What does it mean for a soul to proclaim the greatness of the Lord? Is it not to take the infinite God and to both magnify and reflect him within the human soul? Such intensity! Such a miracle!

This is precisely what Mary did. She bore the infinite God within her finite and human body. Such an impossibility was made possible through the miracle of a boundless God. God could only be thus bound within a human womb because of his boundless power. That which is infinite is magnified within the finite. That which is invisible is magnified clearly within the visible. That which is unknowable is known within the womb of a poor and simple maiden.

Bonaventure believed that every human soul had the potential to magnify the Lord. He says, "Whenever the mind considers itself it rises through itself as a mirror, to the vision of the Holy Trinity. . . . Entering within itself, the soul enters the heavenly Jerusalem where, beholding the choirs of angels, it sees in them God." As the scriptures say of wisdom herself, "She is an aura of the might of God and a pure effusion of the glory of the Almighty. . . . for she is the refulgence of eternal light, the spotless mirror of the power of God, the image of his goodness. . . . Passing into holy souls from age to age." Thus, every human soul has the potential of magnifying the Lord and visibly reflecting the invisible.

Bonaventure sees this paradox as perfectly accomplished in the Virgin's womb through Christ. "For in him the First Principle is united with the last to be created; God is united with man formed on the sixth day; eternity is united with time-bound humanity, with a Man born of a Virgin in the fullness of the ages; utter simplicity is united with the most composite, pure action with supreme passion and death, absolute perfection and immensity with lowliness, the supremely one and all inclusive with an individual composite man, distinct from every other: the Man Jesus Christ."

Why is the magnification and reflection of such a mystery not possible within us all? Bonaventure says it is simply because of sin and the lack of grace. "Let us not believe that it is enough to . . . strive without divine grace or to reflect as a mirror without divinely inspired wisdom . . . I am supposing that the mirror of the outside world is of little or no value, useless, if the mirror of the mind is not clear and polished. Therefore, man of God, train yourself by heeding the sharp goad of conscience before you lift your eyes to the beam of wisdom reflected in the mirrors of the same wisdom, lest you fall into a deeper pit of darkness for having gazed upon such light." We must polish the mirror of our own soul through repentance of sin and acceptance of divine grace in Jesus. Then, like Mary, our soul will also magnify the Lord.

Do we realize the mystical wonder possible within our own soul? Do we realize that our feeble human soul can literally magnify the greatness of the Lord? What a privilege and a challenge! Yet it is not impossible even for the most lowly among us, as long as we receive these divine wonders in humility. Only by humbly admitting that we will never totally comprehend the incomprehensible, will our soul ever join with the humble Virgin Mary in reflecting and magnifying the infinite through the finite. Very God through our own human flesh.   □

Obedience Sets Us Free
Luke 1:57-66 (December 23)

At that moment his mouth was opened and his tongue loosed, and he began to speak in praise of God. (v. 64)

How obedience sets us free! Contrary to limiting our freedom, obedience gives direction to our life. This direction helps us to accomplish great things. It is much like the old example of the train and the train track: The train has power on its own, but without the track it cannot go anywhere. Only when it keeps its wheels on the track can it travel speedily, safely and smoothly. If even one of its wheels comes off the track, the safety of the train and everyone in it is jeopardized. So it is with obedience: if our love is directed by obedience to

God's truth, we can accomplish great things. Love without the truth is misdirected and often frustrated in its attempts to reach its goal. Truth without love is empty and pointless. Likewise, if even one area of our life of love remains off the track of God's truth, it will slow us down, make our journey rough, and even threaten to wreck our entire life.

In today's gospel, Zechariah corrects the disobedience which struck him mute, by an obedience which loosened his tongue. Even though chastised by God for a time, he remained faithful and obedient, so his tongue was loosened and his mouth opened. What disobedience silenced, obedience healed so that God's praises would again be heard from a man of God.

Such praise is a theme throughout the infancy narratives. Zechariah "speaks in praise of God" and goes on to be filled with the Spirit. Elizabeth "was filled with the Spirit and cried out in a loud voice: 'Blest are you among women and blest is the fruit of your womb.'" Mary responds, "My being proclaims the greatness of the Lord . . . holy is his name."

Notice, too, the connection between this praise and the presence of the Holy Spirit. The Spirit overshadows Mary so she magnifies the greatness of the Lord and conceives God's Son in her human womb. The Spirit is with John the Baptist from the womb so that even in the womb he leaps up to God in response to the visit of Mary, who carries God's Son in her own womb. Elizabeth responds to the Spirit-filled leap of the child in her own womb and blesses both Mary and the Divine Fruit of Mary's womb.

Only Zechariah is not at first filled with the Spirit. Only Zechariah, man of God that he was, did not obey the angel in total faith. Only Zechariah is struck mute by the angel of the Lord. Only with Zechariah's final obedience was he, too, filled with the Holy Spirit. He then went on to praise God and to utter a powerful prophecy about his Spirit-filled son, John.

We see a connection between obedience, praise and being filled with the Holy Spirit. We can stifle the Spirit by disobedience and doubt. We can also stir up the Spirit through obedience and praise. Through the working of the Spirit in our life, great miracles take place. Things that seem impossible by human standards become possible, for nothing is impossible with God. Jesus himself is born into the world, even through our weak and human life. As Francis says, "On all those who do this and endure to the last the Spirit of God will rest. It is they who are the brides, the brothers and the mothers of our Lord Jesus Christ."

Do we really see obedience to God's truth as a way to release the power of the Holy Spirit in our life? Or do we see obedience to God as limitation of our human freedom? Do we live our life in an attitude of skepticism and doubt, or do we live in a positive attitude of thanksgiving and praise? Both obedience and praise stir up the gift of the Spirit in our life. Today, if you face seemingly impossible situations, be first obedient and then begin to praise and thank God. Then God will do something great and impossible; he will work the greatest of all miracles, the birth of Jesus into every situation of our life! ☐

The Spirit Is Poured Out
Luke 1:67-79 (December 24)

Then Zechariah his father, filled with the Holy Spirit, uttered this prophecy. (v. 67)

Finally we see even Zechariah filled with the Holy Spirit. In all the infancy narratives we see a direct connection between being obedient and being filled with the Spirit. Mary, especially, is overshadowed by the Spirit of God in union with her fiat, her "Be it done unto me according to your word."

Zechariah's prophecy fulfills the prophet Joel concerning the outpouring of the Spirit: "I will pour out a portion of my Spirit on all mankind: Your sons and daughters shall prophesy, your young men shall see visions and your old men shall dream dreams. Yes, even on my servants and handmaids I will pour out a portion of my Spirit in those days, and they shall prophesy." This is fulfilled in connection even with the birth of Jesus. Elizabeth, Zechariah, Mary, Anna, and Simeon—all were filled with the Spirit. All praised God and prophesied!

Zechariah's prophecy itself roots the exciting work of the Spirit in the present with the work of the Spirit in the past. The ministry of John will both continue and fulfill the ministry of the prophets of the past while heralding the prophetic work of Christ in the future. As 2 Peter says, "Prophecy has never been put forward by man's willing it. It is rather that men impelled by the Holy Spirit have spoken under God's influence." If we are in touch with the Spirit today, we will also be in harmony with the work of the Spirit in the past. According to the Book of Hebrews, "Jesus Christ is the same yesterday, today, and forever."

Another important note is that Zechariah's prophecy comes after "his mouth was opened and his tongue loosed." This is strikingly similar to the description of the experience of the first Christians at Pentecost. Even as Peter quoted the prophet Joel in connection with the pentecostal manifestation of the Spirit, so does Zechariah fulfill the prophecy of Joel in an experience that points towards the loosing of all our tongues at Pentecost.

This has much to say to a Christianity where the average church service is often formal, restricted and dull. We are not rooted in the past in the same way that Zechariah and John were. Instead, we are so rooted in the past that we are unable to move at all! No one opens their mouth unless to do so conforms to the formal, written liturgy. If there is any spontaneity, it is on the part of the minister or priest. Like Zechariah we need our tongues loosed and our mute mouths opened in order to fully praise God. Like Zechariah we need to be obedient to the word of the Lord which encourages us to such praise before the Spirit will fully fall upon our lives and our community.

Are we afraid of spontaneous praise? In attempting to fulfill the old have we only fallen into a ritualistic rut? Let us obey God, praise God, and then be filled with the Spirit of God who inspired the prophets of old. □

Jesus Comes to the Lowly
Luke 2:1-14 (Midnight, December 25)

She gave birth to her firstborn son and wrapped him in swaddling clothes and laid him in a manger, because there was no room for them in the place where travelers lodged. (v. 7)

Jesus is born in a stable, a stable he did not even own. He who dwelt in heaven came to us in a stable. He whose heavenly Father created the splendor of the universe, came to us lowly and homeless. He lived his life in exactly the same way: "The Son of Man has nowhere to lay his head." He entered the kingly city of Jerusalem "lowly, riding a colt." Jesus is at birth what he will be all his life.

He comes, not to the wealthy and influential, but to simple shepherds. Had Jesus wished to come in glory, even the glories of Jerusalem or Rome itself would have waned pale by comparison. The only way to reveal the mystery of his glory was to come to earth dwelling among the lowly. So is Jesus born for the shepherds to see.

Shepherds are contemplatives. They spend long hours simply watching. They are essentially solitary, living in the wilderness around a town or village. Their life is slow paced, with time to contemplate, because they contemplate they care.

The shepherds themselves may have understood Jesus' mission better than anyone on earth. They spent long hours watching their flocks. Their sheep were beautiful, but helpless. Without the constant care of a shepherd sheep will be easily attacked by predators or even walk right over the edge of a cliff. Many would wander off alone and be lost were it not for the shepherd who seeks out the one lost sheep and brings it home to the flock. Further, sheep require daily, individual attention and love. Every day the Good Shepherd pets each sheep, lest the sheep feel alone or lose heart and the will to live. Sheep are so much like people. Shepherds understood the work of this Messiah better than kings, priests, or princes. The Good Shepherd came to dwell among the meek and lowly people of God.

The angels give witness to the manifestation of the awesome mystery of God in this birth. "Glory to God in the highest and peace to those of good will" they proclaimed. God's glory is manifested in a scene so humble. God's total manifestation on earth is clearly revealed in such obscurity. The greatest cities and kingdoms could not contain this glory properly, yet an obscure stable can express the divine mystery better than riches and wealth. The presence of the angels gives witness to this complete manifestation of the mystery of salvation.

Do we find God's glory in such humble settings? Do we join with Jesus who had nowhere to rest his head or do we spend our life looking for an earthly rather than a heavenly home? Do we clamor after the possessions of this materialistic age, or do we follow Jesus? Do we look for Jesus among princes and priests, or do we find him among the simple working class? Do we arrange our life to provide quiet, slow-paced time to contemplate the Good Shepherd, or is our life a non-stop array of fast-paced activity which accomplishes little? Further, do we take the time to treat each other with the genuine respect of a fellow human being, or do we treat one another with very little real concern? The birth of Jesus speaks eloquently of his message and his life. Let us not miss its significance.

Neither should we pass over the significance of the little town of Bethlehem, nor the census that took Joseph and Mary there.

Bethlehem is not only the kingly city of David. It is called the "house of bread." How fitting that the "Bread of Life" was born in that city. How fitting that this king of peace would give his own life, his own flesh, to feed the poor with bread. He who would spiritually feed the world with the sacrifice of his flesh was born in the "house of bread." As Bede says, "Even to the end of the world the Lord would not cease to be conceived at Nazareth and born in Bethlehem, as often as any one of those who hear Him, taking the flour of His Word, make unto themselves a House of Eternal Bread. Daily in the virginal womb, that is, in the soul of the faithful, is he conceived by faith, and brought forth by baptism."

Consider the census: "In those days Ceasar Augustus published a decree ordering a census of the whole world." Jesus is born during a census of the whole world so that the whole world can be saved. The King of Kings is enrolled in the census of an earthly king to bring all the kingdoms of earth to the kingdom of heaven! One ancient commentary says it this way: "Christ was enrolled in the census of the whole world, so that He might sanctify all men; and He was recorded with the whole world, that He might unite all men in Himself." Joseph and Mary obey the law of justice so that all who follow their Son might be justified by faith and enroll themselves in the work of justice.

Bede says this of Jesus' crib: "He, whose throne is in the heavens, confined to the narrowness of a crib, so that he might open wide to us the joys of his eternal kingdom. He that is the Bread of Angels reclines in a manger, that we as sanctified beasts might be fed the corn of his flesh." And Cyril says: "He found that man had become a beast in his soul, and so he is placed in the manger, in the place of fodder, that we, changing from our animal way of living, may be led back to the wisdom that becomes humanity: stretching out, not towards animal fodder, but to the heavenly Bread for the life of this body."

Let us turn from our beastly ways and turn to the God who shows us what it is to be human again. Let us feed those who hunger with the Bread come down from heaven. Let us give shelter to the homeless with him who could first find no room in the inn. Let us welcome him into the inn of our lives, so we might be fully alive, fully human again!   □

We Have to Choose
Luke 2:15-20 (Dawn, December 25)

They [the shepherds] went in haste and found Mary and Joseph, and the baby lying in the manger; once they saw, they understood what had been told them concerning this child. . . . Mary treasured all these things and reflected on them in her heart. (v. 16-17, 19)

The shepherds went in haste. They could not just sit still and find their God. They had to respond! They had to act! Having heard the word of the angel, they had to choose and respond. Otherwise they would never truly understand. As Ambrose says of this text: "No one comes seeking Christ in sloth." As the first disciples responded immediately to the call of Christ, so did the shepherds respond in haste. In this they become the model for the response of all true disciples of Jesus.

We also must choose. As the scriptures say, "There are set before you fire and water, to whichever you choose, stretch forth your hand. Before men are life and death, whichever he chooses shall be given him." We must respond, or we will never find Christ.

Let us not too quickly overlook the response of Mary, the chosen. She responds quietly. She "treasured all these things and reflected on them in her heart." She is the contemplative. She responds in trusting and pliable faith, so she actively gives birth to the Son of God.

Ambrose says, "Let us learn from the Holy Virgin to be chaste in all respects; who no less modest in speech as in person, quietly gathered to her heart all the proofs of her faith." Mary, chosen by God through an angel of the Lord, responds in a song of praise (the Magnificat), gives birth to the Eternally Begotten, and is reduced to a reverent silence.

In Mary we see a pattern for our whole Christian life. We are first chosen of God: for it is "not that we have loved God, but that he first loved us and sent his Son as an offering for our sins." Then we must respond in Spirit-filled thanksgiving and praise saying, "My soul does magnify the Lord." From this praise in the Spirit we thus enthrone the Father and give birth to the eternally begotten Son in our life. In this we are also begotten, for "everyone who loves is begotten of God." We give birth to the Eternally Begotten, and thus are born ourselves. In this we become both mother, and brother or sister of Jesus. This awesome mystery reduces us, with Mary, to divine silence in the presence of the eternal Word.

Do we understand the balance between charismatic praise and contemplative silence? Do we emphasize one to the exclusion of the other? We must respond in active haste and excitement if we are to fully pass over to contemplation. We must be a shepherd if we are to also be Mary. We must be a fool if we are to be wise. Yet let us not always remain the fool. Nor let us think ourselves wise before we have really found the wisdom of being a fool for Christ.   □

Eternally Begotten
John 1:1-18 (Christmas Day, December 25)

In the beginning was the Word; the Word was in God's presence, and the Word was God. . . . The Word became flesh and made his dwelling among us, and we have seen his glory: the glory of an only Son coming from the Father, filled with enduring love. (v. 1, 14)

Here is such a mystery that all the books in the world could not contain it. The infancy narratives and the Christmas gospels are so rich that I am at a loss to emphasize any one point, yet I cannot write about them all. A wonder fills my soul as I contemplate the mystery of the birth of Christ so that I can only weep rather than write.

As St. Bonaventure says: "When our mind contemplates in Christ the Son of God, our own humanity so wonderfully exalted and so ineffably present in Him; and when we thus behold in one and the same Being both the first and the last, the highest and the lowest, the circumference and the center, the Alpha and the Omega, the caused and the cause, the Creator and the creature, then our mind at last reaches a perfect object . . . it reaches with God the perfection of enlightenment. . . . Nothing more is to come but the day of quiet, on which, in ecstatic union, the mind rests after all its labors." Consideration of the mystery of Christmas brings us to charismatic "ecstatic union" when fully considered. Our mind cannot contain the fullness of its perfection, nor attain its perfect simplicity. It must be understood with the ecstacy of the heart!

Today we celebrate that God became flesh. Let us begin here, and thus be led to the eternal. God did not just write in tablets of stone with a divine and mystical finger. He did not just send prophets or angelic messengers. Those things are all wonderful, but not as wonderful as the fact that "the Word was made flesh and dwelt among us." As Hebrews says, "In times past, God spoke in fragmentary and varied ways to our fathers through the prophets; in this, the final age, he has spoken to us through his Son."

The infinite God made himself approachable by taking on finite flesh. So that man might be born of God, God was first born of man through Mary. As Hebrews say, "He became like us, in every way... except sin." Our creed says, "For us men and for our salvation, he came down from heaven. By the power of the Holy Spirit he was born of the Virgin Mary and became man."

Yet this Word, this Son, is not just the Son at his incarnation through Mary. He is "eternally begotten of the Father. God from God, Light from Light, true God from true God. Begotten, not made, One in being with the Father."

Jesus is eternal as Paul says, "He is the image of the invisible God, the firstborn of all creatures. In him everything in heaven and on earth was created, things visible and invisible, whether thrones or dominations, principalities, or powers; all were created through him, and for him. He is before all else that is." Jesus is the Son, and the Son is the Word, and the Word is present to God as the eternally begotten Son of God. He did not begin, or he would not be eternal, so his "begottenness" is not something that happened at a point in time. Yet he must be begotten or he is no Son. Therefore in order to be both eternal and Son, he must be eternally begotten.

Augustine provides these analogies, "Fire gives forth light; light flows out of the fire. . . . Let us consider something born by the reflecting water, a young tree or grass. Is it not born together with its image? The tree and the image both begin together. If the shoot were there always, so also would be its image. That which arises from another, is indeed born. There can therefore be that which forever begets, and that which is forever begotten."

There are many other examples, quotes, and proofs we could use to speak of the life within the Trinity and the beauty of the incarnation. The simplicity of today's gospel, itself, gives birth to the infinity of divine mystery, even though Jesus is clearly manifested as a little, finite, Child in Bethlehem. From this simple scripture spring forth all the mysteries of the Trinity and the incarnation, all the beauties of creation and redemption. One is intimately connected to the other. If one is, then all are. If one is absent, they all cease to be in their present beauty. I mean this quite literally as regards the eternal begottenness of the Son within the Trinity.

Do we fully appreciate the awesome mystery of the eternal begottenness of the Son, the Word? Or do we look on Christmas as the birth, or beginning, of a mere prophet, perhaps the highest human messenger of God? If Jesus is the Word, and the Word is God, then this Son must be eternal! Thus, from the simple human beginnings of an obscure crib we are led to contemplate the highest mysteries of God. These mysteries are not unapproachable. They have been made flesh in Christ. Let us behold and wonder. Let us come to the crib and worship the King. Let us approach the finite and discover the infinite. Let us touch the flesh of Jesus, his body and his blood, and draw near to the untouchable. □

Jesus Divides
Matthew 10:17-22 (December 26)

Brother will hand over brother to death, and the father his child; children will turn against parents and have them put to death. You will be hated by all on account of me. But whoever holds out till the end will escape death. (v. 21-22)

Christmas is so often thought of as a time for family and friends, a time of peace and goodwill. The Holy Family is itself a symbol of the perfect family of peace. Yet here, the day after Christmas, the church calls to our minds and hearts Jesus' solemn warning about division.

The angels announced, "Peace on earth to those on whom his favor rests," yet Jesus also says, "Do not suppose that my mission on earth is to spread peace." The shepherds found Mary and Joseph, and the baby lying in the manger, yet Jesus says, "I have come to set man at odds with his father, a daughter with her mother, a daughter-in-law with her mother-in-law—in short, to make a man's enemies those of his own household."

Jesus is both the divider and the common denominator of the whole human race. He can unite a family more closely than any other, or he can divide it more bitterly. He can bring a peace which passes all understanding, or he can bring war. Why is it that the name of Jesus has brought the greatest peace and the greatest wars in the world?

He unites all believers as a family when he says, "Whoever does the will of my heavenly Father is brother and sister and mother to me." Yet he places this divine family as more important than membership in an earthly family: "Whoever loves father or mother, son or daughter, more than me is not worthy of me. . . . If anyone comes to me without turning his back on his father and mother, his wife and his children, his brothers and his sisters, indeed his very self, he cannot be my follower."

Do we see the Christmas holiday as primarily a family time,

or a church time? Do we see Jesus and our spiritual family as the heart of our celebration, or have we opted for the secular model? Better yet, do we see our primary family as a family of spirit or a family of flesh? It is only in the incarnation of Christ that Jesus binds the two together in love. Yet it is often his incarnate life of love which divides a family right down the middle!

It is really a question of love. Hatred and love cannot co-exist. Hatred must destroy love, for love threatens its very existence. Selfishness will try to destroy selflessness in its need for self-preservation. Thus comes materialism. "You cannot serve both God and money," says the Lord! You must either come out of hatred with love, or slay love with hatred, be selfish or selfless. You cannot be both. Today we must choose which side we are on. Only when our families have been thus divided can the whole world be finally united and healed in love. □

The Holy Race
John 20:2-8 (December 27)

They were running side by side, but then the other disciple outran Peter and reached the tomb first. (v. 4)

Such is the eagerness of the apostles! Such is their love! They hear the news of Mary and immediately run to the tomb of Jesus.

We can learn much by the holy race between the two apostles. John is "the disciple Jesus loved." Peter is the one Jesus chose to build his church upon. In his youthful love, John outruns Peter and reaches the tomb first, but enters in last. John follows Peter. "He saw and believed."

John, one of the "sons of thunder," starts out with zeal, but upon arrival at the tomb sees the linen wrappings on the floor and hesitates. Peter runs more slowly, perhaps more surely, and goes right on in. It is only after following the lead of Peter that John comes to see and believe.

We, too, are called to run a race. Paul says, "Thus do I hope that I may arrive at resurrection from the dead. It is not that I have reached it yet, or have already finished my course; but I am racing to grasp the prize if possible, since I have been grasped by Christ Jesus. Brothers, I do not think of myself as having reached the finish line. I give no thought to what lies behind but push on to what is ahead. My entire attention is on the finish line as I run toward the prize to which God calls me—life on high in Christ Jesus." We run this race within the church, under the leadership of Peter. We might get in front of Peter from time to time, but it will always be Peter who enters the real tomb first, and it will always be by following Peter's lead that we will come to see and believe in the Resurrected Christ in our world.

This holy race should not, however, breed a spirit of competition among us. We should only compete in doing away with worldly competition, which seeks to get ahead at the expense of another.

Do we run the race, or are we content just to walk leisurely after Jesus? Do we start off the moment we hear the word, or do we lag behind? On the other hand, do we start out strong only to lose strength as we approach the finish? How do we run? Do we run with sensitivity to others, or do we seek to run at the expense of another? We must run in love or else we do not run a Christian race at all!   □

For or Against?
Matthew 2:13-18 (December 28)

[Herod] ordered the massacre of all the boys two years old and under in Bethlehem and its environs. (v. 16)

Even the stories of Jesus' birth and childhood proclaim the gospel and call forth a response from the secular world. Since Jesus is the primary model of the church, the history of the church is typified by the historical life of Christ.

Today's gospel symbolizes the tragic persecution period of the early church. Herod hears of Jesus from the visiting men of influence, the astrologers. As soon as those of influence and wealth began to believe in Jesus, those who did not believe became quite nervous. Could this threaten their power, their wealth, their control? Better to kill the innocent than lose control! So kill they did. Just as Herod killed the holy innocents of today's gospel, so did the emperors of Rome slaughter the innocents who followed the way of the Nazarene. The slaughter of the innocents by Herod at Jesus' birth was repeated during the tragic persecution by Rome.

Is there persecution today? There are still rulers and nations that slay the innocent in order to protect their reign of terror and fear. Consider the communist persecution of the church, the bloodshed in Central America, and the terrorism and war in the Mid-East. All who propagate such terror and fear are the Herods of today's world. They are small men defending small ideas by the slaughter of innocent lives. These innocents are those who hold to an ideal of goodness and truth, in faith. They are esteemed as precious by Jesus, the author of all goodness and truth, and their blood will not be shed in vain. It will mingle with the blood of Christ to bring redemption to the whole world.

Who will we support today? Will we support Herod, or will we help the Christ child to escape Herod's slaughter? Will we persecute and oppress, or will we liberate? If we support the Herods of this world, then the blood of the holy innocents of all generations will be on our hands.

Today we must simply look around us. Herod still lives and the innocents can still be saved. The Christ child can escape. We can help all who flee the persecution of governments which violate basic human rights. If we are people of influence we must join with the wise and stately astrologers to help save the Christ child. We must do what we can to save those whom we can. Just look and you will still find Herod and the innocents as close as your own backyard, or as far away as the troubled nations on the other side of the world. But you will find them. And once you find them you must respond.

Your response will manifest your own heart. Does Herod live in your heart, or does the Christ child? If you support the Herods of this world, then the spirit of Herod is within you. If you support the escape of the Christ childs of this world, then the Spirit of Christ dwells within you.

The choice is clear. You are either for Christ or for Herod, with Christ or anti-christ, indwelt by the Spirit or indwelt by the devil. Today's gospel tells the story of a slaughter long ago, but it calls us to make choices today. Make the choices. Then discover what spirit really dwells within your heart. I pray the Spirit of the Christ child is within you all.   □

We Are Co-Heirs with Christ
Luke 2:22-35 (December 29)

This child is destined to be the downfall and the rise of many in Israel, a sign that will be opposed—and you yourself shall be pierced with a sword—so that the thoughts of many hearts may be laid bare. (v. 34-35)

Here the prophet Simeon, inspired by the Spirit, prophesies regarding the saving work of Jesus on the cross. A Messiah for Israel? Yes. "It was revealed to [Simeon] by the Holy Spirit that he would not experience death until he had seen the Anointed of the Lord." But this Child who fulfilled this promise to Simeon was not to be the glorious conqueror accepted by all the Jews. He would be a stumbling block, a sign of confusion, and a revealer of consciences and hearts.

It is the preaching of the cross which causes these things. Paul says, "We preach Christ crucified—a stumbling block to the Jews and an absurdity to Gentiles."

The wisdom of the Spirit puts the world to confusion, though it brings the church to perfect harmony and order.

Paul continues. "I did not come proclaiming God's testimony with any particular eloquence of 'wisdom.' No, I determined that while I was with you I would speak of nothing but Jesus Christ and him crucified. . . . My message and my preaching had none of the persuasive force of 'wise' argumentation, but the convincing power of the Spirit." The Spirit is like "a wind that blows where it wills" defying strict legality and organization. But Paul also says of the use of spiritual gifts, "Make sure that everything is done properly and in order." The Spirit cannot be confined by the logic of man, but it brings ultimate peace, harmony, and order in its supernatural power.

Both the cross and the Spirit are "a sign that will be opposed." They also lay the "thoughts of many hearts bare." Paul goes on, "Who, for example, knows a man's innermost self but the man's own spirit within him? Similarly, no one knows what lies at the depths of God but the Spirit of God. . . .The natural man does not accept what is taught by the Spirit of God. . . .The spiritual man, on the other hand, can appraise everything, though he himself can be appraised by no one."

This truth drives the natural world crazy. The world desires to understand everything it sees, but neither the mystery of the cross nor the wind of the Spirit can ever be totally understood. Jesus simply did not fit into the pattern of the world. His love was contrary to the logic of the Gentiles, and his cross was a sign of defeat for the sign-seeking Jews. Both were scandalized and confused by this itinerant preacher from Nazareth who dared to call himself the Son of God, the Messiah.

Simeon also prophesies to Mary: "A sword shall pierce your heart." Mary was important to the plan of God. She was obviously with Jesus at his birth. She was with him at the first miracle. She was with him during much of his ministry. Likewise, she was with him at the foot of the cross. Further, she was a witness to his resurrection, and was in the upper room at the outpouring of the Spirit in tongues of fire at Pentecost. Mary shares as much as is humanly possible in the saving world of the Son of God. As Paul says, "God sent forth his Son born of a woman." That Son was Jesus. That woman was Mary.

Is it really so strange she would be considered so integral to the plan of Christ? Are we not all co-heirs with Christ? Did not Paul say, "In my own flesh I fill up what is lacking in the sufferings of Christ for the sake of his body, the church"? Don't we all share in the work of the Lamb of God who takes away the sins of the world? Mary shared in both the Spirit and the sufferings of her Son, and it is these two things which bring salvation to the world.

What of us? The symbol of "the woman clothed with the sun" applies not only to Mary, but to the whole church. Do we fully share in the saving mystery of Christ through the sufferings we bear? Do we share in the work of the Spirit? Do we try to make things so logical in the church that we see the working of the Spirit only as confusion? Do we try to become so powerful in the church and in the politics of the world that we see the cross only as defeat and foolishness? We must be like Mary so we can be like Christ. We must be silent and hidden, even within the life of the church, so that only Jesus will be seen and heard. A sword must also pierce our heart, or we can bring healing and peace to no one. We must be "pierced" by the sword of the cross if we are to be fully impregnated by the Spirit. The Spirit must impregnate our life, or we will never give birth to the harmony and true wisdom of God. □

Anna, Prophetess of God
Luke 2:26-40 (December 30)

She was constantly in the temple, worshiping day and night in fasting and prayer. (v. 37)

Anna stands as a symbol of hope to all who have suffered the loss of love. She was a widow. Today's gospel says, "She had seen many days, having lived seven years with her husband after her marriage and then as a widow until she was eighty-four."

Anna did not let either her age or the loss of her husband prevent her from living her life fully. She did not curl up and die. To her, the death of her husband must have seemed yet a new beginning within the many new beginnings of life. Instead of an obstacle, she saw this personal tragedy as an opportunity to draw closer to God. And she did, in fact, become a prophetess of God.

Paul speaks of two kinds of widows in his letter to Timothy: "The real widow, left destitute, is one who has set her hope on God and continues night and day in supplications and prayers. A widow who gives herself up to selfish indulgence, however, leads a life of living death." He goes on about the latter: "They learn to be ladies of leisure, who go about from house to house becoming not only time wasters but gossips and busybodies as well, talking about things they ought not to. . . . Already some here turned aside to follow Satan."

The widow has a choice to make. She has great opportunities before her as she faces a new life. She can either use those opportunities for good or for evil. Likewise, she can choose between the good and the better as she faces the possibility of a life of celibacy and solitude.

Paul says, "The one who marries does good, the one who does not will do better." Yet he also says of widows, "Refuse to enroll the younger widows, for when their passions estrange them from Christ they will want to marry. This will bring them condemnations for breaking their first pledge." Because so many widows become "gossips and busybodies. . . . I should like to see the younger ones marry, have children, keep house, and in general give our enemies no occasion to speak ill of us." Paul realizes the high possibilities for the celibate and solitary widow, even alluding to the early church practice of enrolling the widows into an "order" of sorts with a vow. But he also recognizes the very real human needs and frailties which might suit one better for remarriage.

Today a challenge is laid before all who suffer the loss of a loved one and find themselves alone. You can either serve God without compromise or fall back into the ways of the world. You may choose celibacy or remarriage, but you still must choose to follow Jesus radically or not. If you turn away from Christ, you will end up living a life of living death. If you follow Christ radically through constant worship, fasting and prayer, you may well end up a prophetess of God! ☐

We Shall See Him Face to Face
John 1:1-18 (December 31)

No one has ever seen God. It is God the only Son, ever at the Father's side, who has revealed him. (v. 18)

Here is the great mystery of the incarnation again stated. Likewise, the mystery of the Holy Trinity is alluded to. We cannot see God, yet he is revealed in Jesus. The Son is ever at the right hand of the Father in heaven, yet he reveals God in the flesh on earth. This is a paradox. This is divine mystery revealed in Christ.

Moses was so intimate with God that the Lord used to speak to him face to face, as one speaks to another. Yet when Moses was granted his special request to look upon God's glory, God said, "You may see my back; but my face is not to be seen. . . . My face you cannot see, for no man sees me and still lives."

Yet, in Jesus we look upon the face of God. Paul says, "He is the image of the invisible God. . . . It pleased God to make absolute fullness reside in him." God spoke his name to Moses, as "I AM WHO I AM." In John's Gospel Jesus speaks of himself as "I AM," and the crowd responds violently to his seeming blasphemy. Philip said to Jesus, "Show us the Father," and Jesus replied, "After I have been with you all this time, you still do not know me?"

This is a tremendous mystery. In Jesus we look upon the face of God in the face of a human being. We look upon the Creator in the created. We see God's divinity in this humanity, his glory in this humility. We seem to see only a man, but with the eyes of faith we look upon the face of God himself.

Yet we still await the coming of our Lord. This coming is "already" but "not yet." This glory is unveiled, but not fully seen. We still wait to see "the Son of Man coming on the clouds of heaven with power and great glory." Though we are now redeemed and saved, "We await the redemption of our bodies. In hope we are saved." Salvation is already, but not yet. The same holds true for the revelation of glory. Paul says, "Now we see indistinctly, as in a mirror, then we shall see face to face."

Can we see the face of God reflected in the faces of human beings? Do we fully appreciate the mystery of the revelation of the face of God in Christ? Yet even in the midst of our appreciation of the incarnation and the divinity of the human Jesus, do we still look forward to an even more glorious coming? Are we aware that something far better awaits us?

There is more to life than this dreary earthly existence. There is heaven! Once we hope for heaven, then heaven will come down to earth for us daily to change all that is dreary into a glorious miracle of God. Look upon the face of Christ; hope for the glory of Christ, and you will never look upon the face of your fellow human being in quite the same way. Your life will change for the better. □

Mary, Vessel of the Incarnation
Luke 2:16-21 (January 1)

[The shepherds] went in haste and found Mary and Joseph, and the baby lying in the manger. . . . The shepherds returned, glorifying and praising God. (v. 16, 20)

A true understanding of Mary will lead us to Jesus and cause us to give glory to God. Even as the shepherds found Jesus with Mary, so do we who find Jesus also find him coming into the world through Mary. Even as this realization led the shepherds to give glory to God, so should it lead us to glorify and praise God.

Mary is called *Theotokos,* or "God-bearer." This term was first officially used by the church in 431 A.D. at the Council of Ephesus. This particular council was concerned, not so much with Mary, but with the deity of Jesus Christ. Mary is called the Mother of God, not to imply that she is equal to or greater than God, but to emphasize that Jesus, her Son, is God the Son. This does not imply that Mary pre-existed God, or that she cosmically gave birth to God. This would destroy God's timeless and eternal nature, and elevate Mary to actually take the place of God. Mary gives birth on earth to the Son who is eternally begotten of the Father in heaven. Mary is the vessel for the incarnation on earth of what happens eternally within the Trinity in heaven. Mary is only important because Jesus is more important.

As Paul says, "God sent his Son born of a woman, born under the law, to deliver from the law those who were subjected to it, so that we might receive our status as adopted sons." Mary gives birth to the Eternally Begotten, so that all the world might be begotten of God. Mary gives birth in time to him who pre-existed from all eternity, so that all the world might know him eternally in the future. Mary gives birth to the Eternal to deliver all who are enslaved in time so that they might enjoy the glorious freedom of a timeless eternity. This is an awesome mystery of our faith, and Mary is a vital part of its unfolding and revelation.

These cosmic mysteries of Christ are referred to in scripture. Of the Son's eternal pre-existence John says, "In the beginning was the Word; the Word was in God's presence, and the Word was God. . . . The Word became flesh and made his dwelling among us." Hebrews says, "In this, the final age, he has spoken to us through his Son, whom he has made heir of all things and through whom he first created the universe. This

Son is the reflection of the Father's glory, the exact representation of the Father's being, and he sustains all things by his powerful word." Thus Augustine spoke of the eternal begottenness of the Son in terms of a reflection of the Father. As Paul says, "He is the image of the invisible God . . . he is before all else that is."

Does our understanding and devotion to Mary lead us to these awesome mysteries of God? Does our meditation on the incarnation of Christ through Mary lead us to the Eternal Begottenness from the Father? Does this lead us to the ever-inspiring mystery of the Trinity itself? If our devotion to Mary does not lead us to contemplate such divine mysteries, then perhaps our devotion to her is not as full or true as it should be. ☐

Are We Like Christ?
John 1:19-28 (January 2)

The testimony John gave when the Jews sent priests and Levites from Jerusalem to ask, "Who are you?" was the direct statement, "I am not the Messiah." They questioned him further, "Who, then? Elijah?" "I am not Elijah," he answered. "Are you the Prophet?" "No," he replied. (v. 19-22)

What a difference exists between John the Baptist and Jesus, even though they were cousins. It's true that much of John's teaching in the Gospel of Luke bears great similarity to the teachings of Jesus. But John directly denies that he is the Messiah whereas Jesus makes this claim very directly and clearly.

Remember the Samaritan woman who said to Jesus, "I know there is a Messiah coming. When he comes he will tell us everything." Jesus replied to her, "I who speak to you am he." Before the Sanhedrin, Jesus was directly asked, "Are you the Messiah, the Son of the Blessed One?" Jesus again replied, "I am; and you will see the Son of Man seated at the right hand of the Power and coming with the clouds of heaven."

No prophet would dare make such claims! John the Baptist did not. Elijah did not. Even Moses, especially Moses, did not. Jesus says of John: "History has not known a man born of woman greater than John the Baptizer. . . . All the prophets as well as the law spoke prophetically until John. If you are prepared to accept it, he is Elijah, the one who was certain to come." Yet John the Baptist dared not make the same claims as Jesus.

Jesus is greater than a prophet and greater than the law. He is certainly greater than the Levites and priests who questioned John. As the Samaritan woman said of the Messiah, "When he comes, he will tell us everything." Jesus tells us everything the human race needs to know about God. As Paul says, "It pleased God to make absolute fullness reside in him."

Yet Jesus tells us something more about John that directly concerns us: "Yet the least born into the kingdom of God is greater than he." Do we realize the ramifications of this statement? If we do, it will shake our entire life. John the Baptist is greater than anyone born into history until Jesus, and all who follow the way of Jesus will be greater than John. We are greater than any of the prophets. We are greater than the law. We are greater than the wisest sage. All this is implied in the name "Christian," or "like Christ."

Are we ready to live up to the title we bear? Do we realize that simply to be a Christian is the greatest title and call possible on the face of the earth today? There is no greater honor. No greater call. No greater challenge. Let us live out what our name and title implies and we will shake the whole world. With John, let us lay aside even our own prophetic ministry and simply follow Jesus Christ. There is no greater vocation possible for us. □

Do We Recognize Him?
John 1:29-34 (January 3)

After me is to come a man who ranks ahead of me, because he was before me. I confess I did not recognize him. (v. 30-31)

Even John the Baptist, the greatest person ever born of woman until Jesus, could not perceive the greatness of the mystery. John says Jesus is "after me, ahead of me and before me." Jesus is all around him, yet he could not perceive him.

Jesus is after John in time, yet ahead of John in eternity. Paul says, "God sent forth his Son born of a woman." Luke's Gospel places Jesus' conception and birth after that of John the Baptist. As the angel said to Mary, "Know that Elizabeth your kinswoman has conceived a son in her old age." Yet even in the womb John the Baptist intuitively recognized the pre-eminence of Jesus. Said Elizabeth to Mary, "The moment your greeting sounded in my ears, the baby leapt for joy in my womb." Likewise, John's ministry precedes the ministry of Jesus in time, but not in importance. "He must increase, but I must decrease," says John of Jesus. Yet Jesus even precedes all of creation in eternity. This is a great spiritual mystery: that the Eternally Begotten would be begotten in time to bring all creation to the glory of the Eternal and the Timeless. As Jesus says of himself in the Apocalypse, "I am the Alpha and the Omega, the First and the Last, the Beginning and the End." Or to the Jews who questioned him about his origins, "I solemnly declare it: before Abraham came to be, I AM." Jesus claims to be the Eternal, he who IS, he who is undenied being.

Why do we fail to perceive these things? Bonaventure says, "Strange is the blindness of the mind, for it fails to attend to the first thing it sees, without which nothing can be known. But as the eye, concentrating on the various distinctions of color, fails to notice the very light by which all are seen. . . . When we face the very light of highest Being, not realizing that this supreme Darkness is actually the Light of our mind, we think we are seeing nothing. The same thing happens

when our eyes gaze upo⸴   ⸴t we are not
seeing anything."

John needed to see the Spirit ⸴   ⸴ Jesus
before he recognized God's chosen   ⸴s we
perceive the working of the invisib⸴   ⸴
today's visible and finite world? Are we ⸴
because we are so used to the cluttered v⸴
purify our perceiveable life, so we may al⸴
Invisible and the Pure. Then we will begin t⸴
Infinite Creator in all the things and people of t⸴
created world. □

Follow the Master
John 1:35-42 (January 4)

*When Jesus turned around and noticed them following him, he
asked them, "What are you looking for?" They said to him, "Rabbi
(which means Teacher), where do you stay?" "Come and see," he
answered. So they went to see where he was lodged, and stayed with
him that day.* (v. 38-39)

This passage is the basis for the traditional monastic
question: "What do you seek?" Centuries ago, all those who
wanted to join a monastery were first left outside the door for
three to ten days to test the seriousness of their call and their
resolve. If they lasted, they were admitted. The elder or abbot
of the monastery would then ask, "What do you seek?" This
marked the beginning of their life and time of training in the
monastery. Only after this time of training could they profess
obedience as permanent members of the community.

Likewise, Jesus' response is based on the tradition of the
Jewish rabbis. When a question was asked of a rabbi, he would
respond, "Come and see." The rabbi would then proceed to
explain the answer to the question in a personal and careful
way.

This approach bears a certain similarity to the philosophical schools of the Greeks. When a pupil studied under a master, he did not simply attend classes in a classroom. He actually took up residence with the master philosopher. Master and pupils would take long walks together during which the teacher would talk to his students. Thus the school was an actual community and the classroom consisted of day-to-day life of the teacher. The students or disciples merely lived with their teacher. That was education enough.

What does this say of our Christian communities? Are they really places where young members can learn from the living wisdom of their elders, or is there a deep and wide chasm between what we know and what we live? Is our knowledge really life changing? Does our theology bring personal conversion?

If not, then it is really not in conformity to the way of Jesus as depicted in today's gospel. Jesus teaches personally. He teaches from the perspective of daily and active life. He simply invites his disciples to accompany him on his way. That was training enough. Is the gospel we preach too complicated for this? Is it life changing enough for this? If it is "like-Christ," then it will properly prepare the apostles of the future to meet the challenges of living for Christ and following in his steps. ☐

Judge According to the Spirit
John 1:43-52 (January 5)

Can anything good come from Nazareth? (v. 46)

How frequently we respond like this. Can anything good come out of this town or that town? Or more likely, can anything good come out of this or that person? Everything seems so familiar, so mundane, so ordinary. How can anything extraordinary come out of the person or place we think we know so well?

The Jewish people did the same thing with Jesus. As the

Gospel of Matthew says, "Where did this man get such wisdom and miraculous powers? Isn't this the carpenter's son? Isn't Mary known to be his mother and James, Joseph, Simon, and Judas his brothers? Aren't his sisters our neighbors? Where did he get all this?" They could not accept the extraordinary things of God as long as these came through ordinary people and places. As the Gospel says, "They found him altogether too much for them."

They assumed they knew Jesus, but they did not. They assumed he was only from Nazareth. They assumed he was only a Galilean: They said, "Look it up. You will not find the Prophet coming from Galilee." They assumed they knew it all, but they did not. They read the scriptures correctly, but they misread Jesus, the author of the scriptures.

Of course, we know that Jesus came forth from Bethlehem. His birth there fulfilled the well-known prophecy concerning the coming of the Messiah, "And you, Bethlehem, land of Judah, are by no means least among the princes of Judah, since from you shall come a ruler who is to shepherd my people Israel." Or as Micah 5:2 says, "From you shall come forth for me one who is to be ruler in Israel; Whose origin is from of old, from ancient times."

As Jesus says of his spiritual origins, "So you know me, and you know my origins? The truth is, I have not come of myself. I was sent by One who has the right to send, and him you do not know. I know him because it is from him I come: he sent me." As to his vast spiritual wisdom: "The Jews were filled with amazement and said, 'How did this man get his education when he had no teacher?' This was Jesus' answer: 'My doctrine is not my own; it comes from him who sent me.'" Jesus shows them that, not only was their judgment about earthly origins incorrect, their spiritual judgment was wrong as well.

What about our perceptions of Jesus? Do we see the extraordinary working of Jesus through ordinary people? Do we misjudge circumstances because we do not wait to know all the facts first? As Sirach says about judging another too quickly, "Admonish your friend—he may not have done it; and if he did, he may not do it again. Admonish your neighbor—he may not have said it; and if he did, that he may not say it again. Admonish your friend—often it may be slander; every story you must not believe." We should not judge by appearance, but make an honest judgment. Furthermore, are we really sensitive to the cosmic origins of the Spirit, or do we judge everything according to externals? Remember: "The wind blows where it will. You hear the sound it makes but you do not know where it comes from. . . . So it is with everyone begotten by the Spirit." Do we judge according to the Spirit or the flesh? In Jesus' day they misjudged him because they judged according to the flesh. Even this they did poorly. Let us not make the same mistake today. □

Other Books of Interest

Let the Fire Fall
Michael Scanlan, T.O.R.

Tells how the power of the Holy Spirit revolutionized the life of Father Mike Scanlan. "Let the reader beware. This is no simple autobiography. It is a bold proclamation of the catching force of the Holy Spirit in the world today, affirming that indeed God is in search of man. *Let the Fire Fall* is testimony to the spiritual truth that all members of the body of Christ—the prominent and the obscure—can be faithful vessels of the loving, healing, redeeming presence of the Holy Spirit."—Senator Mark Hatfield. *$6.95*

Making Sense Out of Suffering
Peter Kreeft

This book is for anyone who has ever wept and wondered, "Why?" Peter Kreeft observes that our world is full of billions of normal lives which have been touched by apparently pointless and random suffering. He then records the results of his own wrestling match with God as he struggles to make sense out of this pain and suffering. "Peter Kreeft takes up the unanswerable and carries us inexorably to the stunning answer."—Elisabeth Elliot, author of *Through Gates of Splendor*. *$6.95*

Available at your Christian bookstore or from:
**Servant Publications • Dept. 209 • P.O. Box 7455
Ann Arbor, Michigan 48107**
Please include payment plus $.75 per book
for postage and handling.
*Send for our FREE catalog of Christian
books, music, and cassettes.*